A Teen
Eating Disorder
Prevention
Book

Understanding Sports and Eating Disorders

Debbie Stanley

THE ROSEN PUBLISHING GROUP, INC.
NEW YORK

Published in 2000 by The Rosen Publishing Group, Inc.
29 East 21st Street, New York, NY 10010

First Edition

Library of Congress Cataloging-in-Publication Data

Stanley, Debbie
    Understanding sports and eating disorders / Debbie Stanley. -
       118 p. : 23 cm. - (A teen eating disorder presention book)
    Includes bibliographical references and index.
    Summary: Describes how the pressures of sports can contribute to the onset of eating disorders such as anorexia nervosa, bulimia nervosa, and binge eating disorder.
    ISBN 0-8239-2993-0
    1. Eating disorders - Juvenile literature 2. Sports - Health aspects - Juvenile literature [1. Eating disorders 2. Sports - Health aspects] I. Title II. Series
    RC552.E18S73 1999
    616.85'26 - dc21   99-49665

Manufactured in the United States of America

ABOUT THE AUTHOR

Debbie Stanley has a bachelor's degree in journalism and a master's degree in industrial and organizational psychology.

*To the athletes
mentioned in this book who died in pursuit of
perfection—Heidi Guenther, Christy Henrich,
Joe LaRosa, Jeff Reese, Billy Jack Saylor—and
to the thousands of others who have fallen victim
to eating disorders.*

Contents

Introduction

Everyone knows that exercise is good for the body. Combined with a well-balanced diet, it is key to maintaining physical as well as mental health. Every day Americans are bombarded with the message that if they don't exercise, they will face serious consequences—from poor health to rejection by friends and family.

It is true that exercise is important to physical health. However, failing to exercise or not being very good at a particular sport are not character flaws. It is unfortunate that the original message—that exercise is valuable to one's health—has been twisted into a scare tactic that helps sell diet supplements, workout gadgets, and gym memberships. That message leaves many people feeling inadequate no matter how fit they are.

Organized sports hold an important place within America's fitness obsession. Our professional athletes are paid millions of dollars for their physical abilities; our champion amateur athletes are hailed

1

as heroes for winning events such as the Rose Bowl and the Olympic Games. Even people who excel at sports on a local level are treated like stars in their schools, communities, and places of employment. Children learn early on that being a member of an athletic team is a good way to earn popularity. Adults see, through events such as company softball games and client golf outings, that athletic prowess is sometimes even rewarded with career advancement.

With so much to gain from fitness and so much to lose without it, it's no wonder that many athletes overexercise or develop eating disorders in an effort to be "the best." But is every person who plays on a team or works out alone at risk? Are some sports more likely to trigger these conditions? Are girls at greater risk than boys? These questions and many others are addressed in this book—and the answers may surprise you.

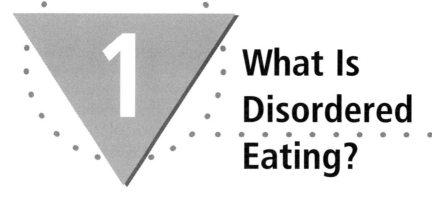

What Is Disordered Eating?

Everyone eats. It's one trait that all living things—humans, animals, even plants—have in common. We all simply must take in nutrients to survive. The means by which we accomplish that, however, vary widely.

When the process is working properly, an organism takes in as much nutrition as it needs and converts it to an adequate amount of energy. In human terms, this means that a person eats as many calories as he or she needs and no more, maintaining an ideal body weight and energy level. Unfortunately, this ideal is rarely achieved. Most people struggle to find the right balance, consuming either too many or too few calories, taking in too much fat and sugar and too few vitamins, and exercising either too much or too little. When the nutritional process is out of balance, the result is called *disordered eating*, and an estimated four out of five people are afflicted by it. Even animals can suffer from disordered eating. When an animal consistently gorges itself and

3

cries for more food, habitually eats plastic, paper, or other substances that are not actually food, or refuses to eat as a result of anxiety, that animal is exhibiting signs of disordered eating.

Anorexia nervosa and bulimia are technically mental disorders, but their consequences are physical. These mental illnesses are responsible for more deaths than any other psychiatric condition. The National Institute of Mental Health (NIMH) reports that one in ten anorexics die from the condition, either from the starvation, from complications such as heart attacks, or from suicide. The overall mortality rate for eating disorder sufferers who do not receive treatment is estimated at 10 to 20 percent. Sufferers are usually adolescent girls and young women between the ages of twelve and twenty-five, although both anorexia and bulima are becoming more common in younger girls and may begin or persist well into adulthood. A growing body of research indicates that the number of male victims is also increasing, but current estimates state that between 90 and 95 percent of eating disorder sufferers are female.

Formal diagnoses of anorexia and bulimia are made based on a set of criteria in the *Diagnostic and Statistical Manual of Mental Disorders* (DSM), a guidebook used by mental health professionals. In order to be considered anorexic according to the DSM, a person must be at least 15 percent lighter than the minimum body weight for his or her height. To be diagnosed a bulimic, he or she must average at least two binge-and-purge sessions per week for at least three months. In addition, other conditions must be met in regard to the victim's self-image and attitude toward food. According to these guidelines, an estimated 1 percent of girls and young women are anorexic and another 2 to 3 percent are bulimic. Also, it is not uncommon for a person to have both anorexia and bulimia; the victim will either progress from one to the other or alternate between the two. And beyond the relatively small percentages mentioned above, it is important to point out that many more people are currently struggling with disordered eating and suffering the physical, mental, and emotional consequences of these diseases, even if they do not yet fit a textbook definition of anorexia or bulimia.

The American Anorexia/Bulimia Association reports that approximately 15 percent of young women have "substantially disordered eating attitudes and behaviors" and more than 5 million Americans are struggling with eating disorders. Of that number, some are anorexic, and others are bulimic or suffer from binge eating disorder (BED). Beyond the three most serious eating disorders, however, are a number of other conditions, including compulsive exercise, malnutrition, fad or yo-yo dieting, smoking, alcohol abuse, drug abuse, depression, and even self-mutilation and obsessive-compulsive disorder, which are correlated in varying degrees with disordered eating.

DISORDERED EATING OR EATING DISORDER?

I have some friends who seem to always be talking about food, and I wonder sometimes which of them could really have a problem. I mean, how can you tell the difference between someone who is really just worried about nutrition and being healthy, and someone who is getting an eating disorder?

Disordered eating is not the same as an eating disorder, such as bulimia, anorexia, or BED. In recent years, researchers studying eating disorders have discovered a wide variety of conditions, traits, and habits that could eventually lead to an eating disorder. This collection of behaviors is now known as disordered eating and is receiving more attention as the effort to prevent eating disorders has grown.

"The new concept of 'disordered eating' emphasizes the spectrum of abnormal eating behavior, with poor nutritional habits on one end, and anorexia and bulimia on the other," Dr. Aurelia Nattiv and Linda Lynch reported in the journal *The Physician and Sportsmedicine.* This broadening of focus has allowed doctors, coaches, and counselors to see other, seemingly less dangerous conditions that could lead to the extremes of anorexia or bulimia. It has also allowed them to recognize that poor eating habits need not be as critical as persistent anorexia or bulimia to be serious and worthy of attention. In her book *Lost for Words: The Psychoanalysis of Anorexia and Bulimia,* Em Farrell estimates that an incredible 80 percent of all people are believed to be affected by borderline disordered eating, known technically as subclinical eating disorder. This means that just 20 percent of all people, or just one in five, have a healthy attitude toward food.

THE DIETING OBSESSION

Just about everyone in my school, guys and girls both, seems to worry about being thin enough. Even the really big guys who play tackle on the football team don't like being teased about their weight. It's not like in that movie Animal House *where the big guys just ate everything in sight; everyone's worried about their weight now.*

Dieting is the most common example of disordered eating. American society today is obsessed with thinness at any price, and the most common reaction to this overwhelming societal pressure is to diet. At its simplest, the idea of dieting is to make a temporary change in one's eating habits to correct weight gain. When the proper weight is achieved, the diet stops.

There is a fundamental flaw in this concept, of course, which has been widely reported: Making a temporary change in one's eating habits to lose weight and then going back to eating "normally" will only lead to gaining weight again. The solution, promoted by nutritionists and doctors, is to make permanent changes in your eating habits so your weight will stay at an ideal point. If you eat a good balance of healthy foods, consume the right number of calories, and exercise according to your individual needs, you shouldn't need to diet.

It sounds simple, but it's not. There is another hidden but very powerful factor involved: the battle of guilt vs. pleasure. The guilt stems from society's insistence that everyone should be model-thin. When a person doesn't measure up to this impossible ideal, he or she feels guilt and shame, and is likely to go on a diet. Dieting the old-fashioned, temporary way eases the conscience because it feels like penance. In the back of his or her mind, the dieter thinks, "If I suffer through this horrible diet and lose some weight, I will be acceptable." The other half of the equation—pleasure—is what prevents people from sticking to a permanent, healthy eating plan.

Ironically, while societal pressure demands that we diet to be thin and therefore acceptable, it also bombards us with the message that we should indulge in every pleasurable thing we can. Every commercial for a soft drink, cereal, candy bar, or restaurant is based on this premise. Our appetites and taste buds have been consistently overwhelmed with fatty, sugary foods, and we have been encouraged to eat and drink everything "just for the taste of it," as one commercial says, and so we choose what to eat based on what sounds good, not on what nutrients we need for the day. With so many "luscious," "rich," and "sinfully delicious" foods to choose from, it's hard to go for the veggies.

GOING TO EXTREMES: EATING DISORDERS

Sometimes disordered eating gets completely out of control and turns into a full-fledged eating disorder, such as anorexia, bulimia, or BED. Each of these conditions has its own unique characteristics, but what they all have in common is that the sufferer has an unhealthy relationship with food.

Anorexia Nervosa

At my worst, no one could convince me that I was too thin. I was positive that they were all just jealous and were trying to make me fat. I'm better now, but I still tend to fall back into my old patterns when I'm overstressed. If I'm not careful, I'll skip meals or exercise too much whenever I'm upset about something.

Anorexia, the deadliest eating disorder, causes its victims to believe that they are overweight, even when it is obvious to others that they are not. The anorexic, who is most often female, avoids food, eating as little as possible, and becomes progressively thinner while her body begins to break down in a number of ways. Her digestion slows, causing constipation. She constantly feels cold, and a thin layer of hair, or *lanugo*, begins to grow all over her body. Her periods stop. She is weak and tired, and may faint frequently. She develops a pasty complexion, and her hair begins to fall out, and she experiences all kinds of side effects that are caused by a lack of certain vitamins and minerals. Her palms and the soles of her feet may turn yellow, and she may bruise or bleed easily.

As the disease progresses, the anorexic's body will begin to break down muscle tissue in order to survive. This leads to liver and kidney damage, and eventually kidney failure, which may kill her or leave her dependent on dialysis for the rest of her life. She may develop osteoporosis, which weakens the bones and makes them break easily. She may be left unable to have children from the effects of the disease. Her heart will also be affected by the breakdown of muscle tissue and the mineral imbalance brought on by anorexia. If her condition remains untreated, she may die of cardiac arrest. In fact, an estimated 10 to 20 percent of anorexics eventually die as a result of the disease.

Bulimia Nervosa

I know it's gross, but it's so common now that my friends and I don't even think about that anymore. We don't do it together, like we don't sit down and pig out together, but we all know that the others sometimes throw up after lunch, especially if it's pizza or something else really fattening.

Bulimia is characterized by alternating episodes of binge eating and purging. A binge may be anything from a bag of chips to a whole bag of groceries, but what every binge has in common is that the sufferer feels out of control and unable to stop eating. The binge stops only when the person is physically unable to eat any more or when his or her feelings of guilt and self-loathing become so strong that the desire to purge takes over.

Purging most often takes the form of vomiting; bulimics make themselves throw up in a desperate attempt to get rid of the food consumed during the binge. While some people stick their fingers down their throats to make themselves vomit, others use dangerous drugs intended to induce vomiting after the accidental ingestion of

YES, YOU CAN HAVE BOTH ANOREXIA AND BULIMIA

As research continues into eating disorders, more is being learned about the coexistence of anorexia and bulimia in the same victim. Experts used to believe that a person could have just one of the two diseases, but now more evidence for the existence of "bulimarexia" or "anorexia/bulimia" is being found. The condition usually manifests itself in alternating cycles of starvation and bingeing/purging. Some experts believe the combination of anorexia and bulimia is even more dangerous to the victim than having just one of the diseases because each damages the body in certain ways.

Perhaps the most well-known victim of anorexia/bulimia is singer and musician Karen Carpenter. She died in 1983 of a heart attack brought on by her struggle with eating disorders. Like many bulimics, she had abused ipecac syrup to induce vomiting for years, and she became progressively thinner and weaker before beginning treatment. Ironically, she seemed to be on the road to recovery when she died; despite her efforts to help herself, her body was simply too damaged to go on.

poison. Some people also abuse laxatives or overexercise to keep themselves from gaining weight after a binge. In addition to bingeing and purging, some bulimics periodically deny themselves food for a day or more, much like anorexics do.

Like anorexia, bulimia is also devastating to the body. Over time, repeated vomiting causes tooth enamel to erode, allowing decay to set in and requiring extensive dental work. The teeth tend to become discolored, particularly the front teeth. Bulimia causes painful, chronic digestive problems—diarrhea and/or constipation, even stomach ulcers. It causes the glands around the face to become enlarged, making the cheeks puffy. When the fingers are used to induce the vomiting, cuts and scarring on the fingers and hands are common. Vomiting causes dehydration and life-threatening imbalances in the body's electrolytes. It can result in menstrual irregularities, kidney damage, irregular heartbeat, and seizures. It can cause death from the damage inflicted on the heart and other organs, from the many chemical imbalances it causes in the body, and from a ruptured stomach or esophagus.

Bulimics also frequently abuse laxatives in an attempt to force the food to rush through their systems without being absorbed. This often leaves them constipated or suffering from such severe diarrhea that they are unable to control their bowel movements at all. Diet pills and diuretics, which rid the body of water, are also popular ways to quickly drop a few pounds, but they also wreak havoc in the body's complex chemical systems.

WHY BULIMIA DOESN'T WORK

The bulimic's goal of being physically perfect is not well-served by purging. Most bulimics believe that when they purge excess calories consumed in a binge, they have prevented themselves from gaining any weight and may even lose weight. But after a while, the body is not so easily outsmarted. Dietitian Joanne Larsen points out in her Web site, "Ask the Dietitian," that "frequent and regular vomiting does not cause weight loss. Your body learns to adjust and starts digesting food higher in the digestive tract because it learns that it can't hold on to the food very long. Also, food stays in the bulimic's stomach much longer because of the frequent vomiting. Bulimic patients have told me of vomiting food they ate almost twenty-four hours before."

Binge Eating Disorder

In elementary school, we sometimes had special lunch days when they brought in McDonald's or pizza, and we had to order halfway through the morning. Well, I always had the biggest order of anyone—five pieces of pizza or five hamburgers. Everyone thought it was funny then. But then one time in high school, when I bought three trays worth of food at lunchtime, I realized that nobody thought it was funny anymore—people actually looked away from me as I walked toward their tables. From then on, I just ate less in public but ate like crazy at home, by myself.

Binge eating disorder is similar to bulimia in that the person is unable to refrain from consuming large amounts of food at one time. The difference between the two is that the sufferer does not purge the food. Therefore, most people suffering from BED, also known as *compulsive eating*, are overweight or obese. An estimated 30 percent of people participating in medically supervised weight-control programs are found to be suffering from BED, compared to an average of 2 percent of the population overall. Like anorexia and bulimia, BED is more common among females than males—approximately 60 percent of its victims are female—but a higher percentage of males suffer from BED than any other eating disorder. BED sufferers feel overwhelming shame at being unable to control their eating and are likely to also have low self-esteem or even depression. It is important to recognize that the inability to keep from overeating is a result of

SOME MYTHS
ABOUT EATING DISORDERS

Myth: Anorexia is a good way to lose weight if you know when to stop.
Fact: Anorexia is an incredibly dangerous way to diet. It is extremely unhealthy and kills between 10 and 20 percent of its victims. Unfortunately, most anorexics start out trying to lose just a few pounds but cannot stop themselves from trying to lose more. Anorexia is not a simple weight-loss technique; it is an emotional illness that leaves its victims powerless to stop it.

Myth: Bulimia is a good way to keep from gaining weight.
Fact: Bulimics do gain weight despite their purging efforts. Most bulimics are at or slightly above their bodies' ideal weight.

Myth: Binge eating is nothing more than a lack of control.
Fact: Everyone has overeaten and regretted it at least once, and then resolved to have better self-control the next time. But people who habitually binge are not weak: They are suffering from binge eating disorder, a psychological disorder similar to anorexia and bulimia. BED victims need and deserve

help and compassion just as much as anorexics and bulimics do.

Myth: People with anorexia or bulimia are self-centered and vain.
Fact: The truth is that people with eating disorders have low self-esteem. Far from being happy with or proud of their appearance, they hate the way they look and believe that losing weight will help. Even when they have lost a large amount of weight and have become dangerously thin, anorexics still see themselves as fat.

Myth: Only girls get eating disorders.
Fact: The vast majority of eating disorder sufferers are female, but the number of male sufferers is steadily increasing. Some researchers believe that there are more male victims than anyone knows about because eating disorders are seen as a girl's problem and boys are reluctant to admit to having them or to seek help.

Myth: Eating disorders are just stubbornness and defiance.
Fact: Belief in this myth is especially common among parents, who see their child's refusal to eat as a discipline problem. It is true that anorexics and bulimics are

attempting to take control through their disease, but not in the way their parents might think. Eating disorder victims feel that their lives are out of control, and they seek comfort by taking charge of their eating. Sometimes it's the only thing in their lives that they can have any control over.

Myth: Eating disorder sufferers are abused at home.
Fact: Unfortunately, some eating disorder sufferers are also victims of physical, psychological, or sexual abuse. There are no conclusive studies to prove that abuse causes eating disorders, or that a larger percentage of abused kids are also anorexic, bulimic, or binge eaters. But researchers have found that an unstable home environment is often the trigger for an eating disorder. This could mean that the victim's parents are getting a divorce, or another child in the family is seriously ill, or the family is having financial problems. It could even mean that some happy event—a sibling's marriage or move to college—is bringing about changes in the family. So although it is possible that an eating disorder victim is being abused, but it is incorrect to assume that all eating disorder sufferers are abused.

Myth: The physical effects of anorexia and bulimia are reversible.

Fact: Much of the damage anorexia inflicts on the body cannot be repaired. Victims who survive anorexia may be left with permanent complications and damage to their hearts, digestive and reproductive systems, and bones. The same is true of bulimics, who are also at high risk for disfiguring dental problems.

Myth: People with anorexia are insane.

Fact: Anorexics suffer from an emotional illness. This is not the same as being insane. However, this myth is common because anorexics have such a skewed body image and obsession with food issues that their thinking and behavior seem strange to others. Also, anorexics are sometimes admitted to hospitals for treatment, which leads some people to the inaccurate assumption that the victim has been committed to a mental institution.

Myth: Anorexics can't stand the sight of food.

Fact: Many anorexics enjoy cooking. They may collect recipes, spend hours in the kitchen preparing gourmet meals for their families, and take great pleasure in watching others enjoy food. Anorexics are chronically hungry, and some find that watching others eat makes their feelings of deprivation more bearable. Preparing food for others also serves as a distraction from the fact that the anorexic is not eating.

Myth: People with anorexia and bulimia are too tired to exercise, so athletes can't have eating disorders.
Fact: Anorexia does sap a person's strength; victims often feel tired, dizzy, or light-headed because they aren't consuming enough calories or liquids to keep their energy levels up. However, many anorexics use exercise as a way to speed up their weight loss, and they will continue to exercise through the pain and fatigue—sometimes even until they faint or collapse. There are many athletes who suffer from eating disorders, and in some cases females develop another serious condition known as the Female Athlete Triad. This is a combination of disordered eating, osteoporosis, and amenorrhea (loss of one's monthly periods).

gluttony or laziness—it is a disease and its sufferers, like those of any other disease, need help to overcome it.

The Sports Connection: Compulsive Exercise

I finally realized that maybe I was obsessed with working out when my parents found me on the treadmill, trying to run even though I had one leg in a cast. I had developed a stress fracture, and it really hurt to put weight on it, so I was leaning on the bars and trying to run on the other leg. My parents acted like they had found me with a gun to my head, but later I realized that they probably had a reason to be concerned.

There is a phenomenon called *compulsive exercise*, which often plays a part in anorexia, bulimia, and BED. While it is not yet considered a separate eating disorder, some researchers believe it should be. Compulsive exercise is a significant problem among athletes and will be discussed throughout this book.

What makes exercise "compulsive"? This question can be hard to answer. Most people find it hard to believe that when it comes to exercise, there can be "too much of a good thing." In the case of a competitive athlete or sports

ANOREXIA AND ATHLETES

When one person suffers from both anorexia and compulsive exercise his or her condition is referred to as anorexia athletica. Risks to the person's health increase.

enthusiast, compulsive exercise is easily disguised as healthy: The compulsive exerciser looks like a motivated, committed athlete with a strong, admirable desire to be the best.

If you exercise regularly or participate in a sport, ask yourself why you do it. Is it because you enjoy the activity, or because you like to win, or because you know that exercise is an important component of overall health? Or is there more to it than that? If you quit your team or skipped your workouts for a while, how would you feel about yourself?

"Signs of obsession include feelings of acute anxiety over a missed workout and an urge to make exercise a priority over friends and family," Alicia Potter noted in an article for the *Boston Phoenix*. "Most trainers recommend working out no more than an hour a day."

Another warning sign, according to Anorexia Nervosa and Related Eating Disorders (ANRED) is "when the activity ceases being fun and becomes a duty, a chore, an obligation that is definitely *not* fun, but that you *must* do—or else suffer strong guilt or anxiety."

If your self-esteem is based largely on your performance in a sport or in your ability to stick to a workout regimen, or if your training program consumes hours every day, gets in the way of relationships with friends and family, interferes with school or work, or involves dangerous prac- tices such as steroid use, you may be headed for a problem with exercise compulsion.

2 Who Has an Eating Disorder?

People used to believe that only young women could have eating disorders, now it is recognized that anyone can fall victim to anorexia, bulimia, binge eating disorder, or compulsive exercise.

FEMALES

The majority of eating disorder sufferers are female. The American Anorexia/Bulimia Association (AABA) reports that 5 percent of adolescent and adult women have anorexia, bulimia, or binge eating disorder. It is hypothesized that the vast majority of eating disorder sufferers are female because society has traditionally placed a much greater burden of physical perfection on women than on men.

It is estimated that 1 of every 250 girls between the ages of twelve and eighteen has struggled with an eating disorder at some time, but it is impossible to know for sure, because not everyone asks for or receives help, and doctors are not required to report the number of eating disorder cases they treat.

The typical anorexic is a white female approximately 15 to 25 percent below her ideal weight and between the ages of twelve and eighteen. Anorexia rarely starts after age twenty-five. The typical bulimic is an average-weight or slightly overweight female between the ages of fifteen and thirty-five. The typical BED sufferer may be male or female.

MALES

Girls and women have always been held to a higher standard of physical beauty than their male counterparts, but that imbalance is changing. Boys and men are beginning to feel much more societal pressure to conform to certain physical ideals. Whereas women have long been expected to look like Barbie and to be ashamed if they could not reach this impossible goal, more and more men are now beginning to believe that their value as a person is based on whether they can look like Ken.

Boys and men have traditionally been left out of most discussions and research on eating disorders, but there is growing evidence that a significant number of males are suffering from them. Alicia Potter reported in the *Boston Phoenix:* "What we do know is that of the eight million Americans being treated for eating disorders, one million are men. According to [psychotherapist T. Donald] Branum, men make up about 10 percent of anorexics and about 20 percent of bulimics. Nearly half of binge eaters are men."

It makes sense that binge eating disorder is so common among males. In American culture, men are expected to have a "healthy appetite," so when a male eats an entire pizza by himself in one sitting, few people see it as a warning sign. If a female were to do that, however, it would likely raise a red flag. Whereas the female would probably be embarrassed and ashamed, the male would be inclined to brag about his feat.

Although the reasons for developing an eating disorder and the ways in which it manifests itself can be different for males and females, in general they spring from the same types of insecurities. One difference that has been noted, however, is the weight of the victim when the eating disorder starts. According to Dr. Arnold Andersen, an expert in the field and author of the book *Males with Eating Disorders,* women often believe they are fat at the onset of an eating disorder, but they are usually near average weight. Men, on the other hand, usually are overweight before the disorder develops.

Many researchers and therapists believe that men are reluctant to seek help for disordered eating because, as Potter noted, "they are ashamed to suffer from a 'woman's illness.' Indeed, the term 'eating disorder' usually conjures the image of a white, suburban teenage girl. But eating disorders among men were documented in medical journals as far back as 1649. It's even suspected that [author] Franz Kafka suffered from anorexia; hence his short story 'The Hunger Artist.'"

Some heterosexual males are also reluctant to seek help for anorexia or bulimia because in recent years the number of homosexual men seeking help for disordered eating has increased; it seems that many straight men are embarrassed to admit to the

STEROIDS ARE STILL POPULAR—AND DANGEROUS

Despite the known danger, the use of anabolic steroids to increase muscle mass remains high, Alicia Potter reported in the *Boston Phoenix*. Potter noted: "About one million men have tried the drugs once; up to 6 percent have taken them by age 18."

Jo Revill reported in an article for This Is London: "In America, where the craze of bodybuilding has gripped thousands of young people, anabolic steroids allow men to attain the shape they want in six months rather than building up their muscles over two years. It is called 'biggerexia'—an obsession that appears to be similar to anorexia, fueled by role models in the film industry."

But that physique comes at too high a price. "There is a long list of health problems that can come with abuse of steroids, which are supposed to be prescribed for the treatment of growth disorders and wasting diseases," Revill noted. "Kidney and liver disorders can be the result, along with heart disease. Now it is thought that steroids can even bring on early arthritis in young men because they put excessive

weight on the joints. The most common
side effect in men, however, is aggression,
or 'roid rage' as it has been dubbed by
some doctors. Coming off the drugs can
cause suicidal thoughts, paranoia and
acute depression."

Steroid use is not limited to males. "In
women," Revill reported, "the drugs can
create hormonal changes that [are] not
possible to reverse, such as a deeper voice,
the growth of body hair, and smaller
breasts."

problem and are afraid that if they seek help they
will be labeled gay. In reality, there is no known cor-
relation between sexual preference and risk of disordered eating; being gay doesn't cause anorexia or
bulimia, and having an eating disorder can't make
anyone "turn gay." This is simply one more myth
about eating disorders.

BEYOND WHITE AMERICANS

Eating disorders were long believed to challenge
only young white women, and some researchers
speculate that, in the past, cultural differences did
indeed protect black, Hispanic, Asian, and Native
American females from anorexia and bulimia. Now,

however, greater numbers of nonwhite females are coming forward to find help for disordered eating. No conclusions have yet been reached on whether this trend indicates an actual rise in eating disorders among nonwhite women or simply an increase in the reporting of them. It is certain, however, that nonwhite women are no longer being ignored as being at risk for eating disorders. Conscientious scientists and doctors recognize that all people, regardless of race, are in danger of developing disordered eating habits as a result of the same societal pressures that afflict whites.

Although the United States reports one of the highest rates of disordered eating in the world, other countries are not immune to the problem. Japan and China have seen a rise in anorexia and bulimia, but the shame associated with psychotherapy in those countries prevents many people from seeking treatment, so accurate measurement or estimation of the extent of the problem there is impossible. Argentina's incidences of both conditions are three times as high as in the United States; the crisis of disordered eating in that country is attributed to a societal obsession with physical perfection that is even worse than America's.

MOST AT RISK

Another group of people are at high risk for eating disorders. The group contains members of all the groups listed previously. That group is athletes, of whom 15 to 62 percent are believed to suffer from eating disorders. That figure is significantly higher than the general population, of which an estimated

1 percent are anorexic and another 2 to 3 percent are bulimic. Some reports suggest that the number of eating-disordered athletes may be even higher. "A recent *Sports Illustrated* article reported that 70 percent of women athletes have eating disorders, and a recent study from a Toronto hospital says that as many as 60 percent of 'seriously anorexic' women were once competitive athletes," Loren Mooney reported in the March 1995 issue of *Cornell Magazine.*

WHICH SPORTS ARE DANGEROUS?

A person can develop an eating disorder while participating in any sport. It's important to realize that it is not the sport itself that causes the eating disorder, but rather the combination of psychological elements in the individual athlete that make him or her vulnerable. Still, some sports have a higher rate of disordered eating than others due to factors within the sport, such as the importance of appearance, the use of weight classes to match opponents, and the advantages (real or perceived) of being lighter than opponents.

Although eating disorders are much more common among females than males in the general population, both genders are at risk in the world of sports. A study of male athletes in Norway revealed that 8 percent of them were suffering from eating disorders and many more were engaged in disordered eating. In the sports of boxing, karate, wrestling, and judo, an incredible 82 percent had used dangerous weight-control methods, such as laxatives, diuretics (water pills), and diet pills.

Wrestling

In the last few years, the weight-cutting practices used by high school and college wrestlers have received a lot of attention and have prompted concern over their effects on the health of the young men using them. Some coaches and wrestlers believe that shedding as many pounds as possible right before a meet in order to compete in a lower weight class is a good way to gain an advantage over opponents. The strategy is dangerous, however, and sometimes fatal. The use of diuretics, rubber suits, steam rooms, and overexercising have been listed as the cause of death for several wrestlers in recent years, and these practices are believed to lead to disordered eating in many more young men.

ESPN *SportsZone's* Tom Farrey reported that at the time of his death, wrestler Joe LaRosa of the University of Wisconsin-LaCrosse "was wearing sweats over a rubber suit and riding an exercise bicycle in a steam-filled shower room. His body temperature ran up to a dangerous 108 degrees." Billy Jack Saylor of North Carolina's Campbell University died while trying to drop six pounds for a match. The University of Michigan's Jeff Reese was wearing a rubber suit and riding a stationary bike when he died of kidney failure and a heart malfunction. Saylor, LaRosa, and Reese died within thirty-two days of each other in 1997.

Many wrestlers reportedly feel invincible and are unafraid to subject their bodies to such extremes, but the message that these practices are dangerous may be getting through. "I don't know how close I am ever to dying," Jade Gribble, a teammate of LaRosa's, commented to Farrey. "I never feel like I'm close, I never put myself in that situation. But yet, I think, how close could I be? I mean, there have been times when I've been tired and not wanted to move. How close is that to how Joe was feeling?"

Cornell wrestling coach Rob Koll says a much better strategy is to build muscle mass through strength training: "We'd like to have a guy get stronger and become a good wrestler rather than a good weight cutter." The National College Athletic Association seems to agree. In 1998, the NCAA introduced new rules intended to curb dangerous weight-cutting practices. The use of saunas and rubber suits or other nonventilated suits is now banned; weigh-in time has been moved from twenty-four hours before a match to just two hours, making it much more difficult to cut weight through dehydration and then rehydration before the match; and a seven-pound cushion has been added to the upper limit for each weight class, meaning, for example, that a wrestler wanting to compete in the 118-pound class can actually weigh up to 125 pounds.

Some wrestlers are disdainful of the new rules, even in light of the deaths of Saylor, LaRosa, and Reese, but legendary University of Iowa wrestling coach Dan Gable has a message for them, as told to Farrey: "They think they're indestructible. But I'll tell you what—

"They think they're indestructible. But . . . those three athletes thought they were indestructible too. And they're not around to talk about it." —University of Iowa Wrestling Coach Dan Gable those three athletes thought they were indestructible too. And they're not around to talk about it."

Dance

Twenty-two-year-old ballerina Heidi Guenther died June 30, 1997, from complications from her eating disorder. Guenther, a well-known dancer with the Boston Ballet, stood five foot three. She was reportedly under ninety-three pounds when she collapsed and died during a family vacation to Disneyland. She had complained for months of "a pounding in her chest," Jon Marcus of the Associated Press reported. "Medical professionals say women with eating disorders often die of heart-rhythm abnormalities that often cannot be detected in autopsies," Marcus noted.

Unfortunately, unrealistic size and weight requirements are common in the dance world; girls are expected to be not just thin, but far below the recommendations of the standard height and weight charts. "People are under pressure to maintain a body weight that is ideal from the standpoint of ballet aesthetics, but not at all ideal from the standpoint of health," Richard Bachrach told Marcus. Bachrach is a doctor of physical medicine and rehabilitation and president of the Center for Dance Medicine, told Marcus.

In her article "Eating Disorders," published online by Suite101.com, Heather Mudgett noted that actress Lea Thompson, star of the TV show *Caroline in the City,* was previously a dancer and was once rejected by a theater company: "At five-foot-five and ninety-six pounds, she was too 'stocky' to be considered."

Running

Distance runners seem to be models of cardiovascular fitness, with lean physiques and amazing endurance. But as in other sports that emphasize low body weight, some runners fall victim to disordered eating in an attempt to improve performance. John Bryant reported in an article for Times Newspapers Ltd.:

> Research at the University of Leeds by Angie Hulley, the former English cross-country champion and marathon international, reveals that one in ten of Britain's female distance runners has "some kind of eating disorder." These runners are obsessively convinced that less fat equals more fitness.
>
> It can happen at the highest level. The current European cross-country champion, Sara Wedlund, is a self-confessed anorexic, while Lucy Hassell, the British international runner, became so thin that she was forced to use a wheelchair. Liz McColgan revealed that in 1988, in the run-up to the Olympics, her weight fell to seven stone [ninety-eight pounds]. She was out-kicked for gold in Seoul. "I was so weak and undernourished I didn't have the energy to sprint for the line," she said.

Gymnastics

Young female athletes are particularly vulnerable to eating disorders when they believe that their performance depends on being thin and world championships are at stake. In a 1988 study, 100 percent of gymnasts surveyed reported being on a diet, 62 percent were using an extreme weight-control method, and 75 percent had been told by their coaches that they had to lose weight. "Although data are lacking," Patty Freedson and Linda Bunker wrote in "Physical Activity and Sport in the Lives of Girls," their report to the President's Council on Physical Fitness and Sports, "it seems reasonable to conclude that adolescent female athletes involved in sports where weight and body fat are predictors of successful performance have an increased risk for developing disordered eating patterns."

Standards have changed: In 1976 the average gymnast was five foot three and weighed 105 pounds. In 1992 the average gymnast was four foot nine and weighed eighty-eight pounds. World-class gymnasts begin training when they are very young, but as they approach adulthood and their bodies begin to change, many girls panic and attempt to avoid puberty, forcing their bodies to stay light and small through eating disorders.

Christy Henrich was a world-class gymnast who died of multiple organ failure in 1994 as a result of her ongoing struggle with anorexia and bulimia. It has been reported that a U.S. gymnastics judge told the four foot ten, ninety-pound teenage athlete that she would have to lose weight if she wanted to make the 1988 U.S. Olympic team. Some people have speculated that this remark was the start of her disordered eating. Christy reportedly weighed less than sixty pounds when she died.

Cathy Rigby, a 1972 Olympian, battled anorexia and bulimia for twelve years. She went into cardiac arrest on two occasions as a result. Other gymnasts, including Nadia Comaneci, have also come forward to discuss their battles with eating disorders.

Figure Skating

Like dancers and gymnasts, the best figure skaters make their sport look easy. The judges and the audience see a handsome young man or beautiful young woman in a glittery (and expensive) costume, flowing smoothly from jump to spin to footwork or skipping playfully through a fast number, all the while making it look like he or she is simply graced with the ability to defy gravity. The reality of the skaters' practices—hard-driving, multihour sessions in which skaters grind through their routines over and over—demonstrates just how important appearance is to the sport. No one wants to see a skater fall, because it destroys the illusion.

That illusion includes a slim physique. All skaters are expected to be thin in order to present the most pleasing image in their form-fitting costumes. As in gymnastics, a skater's appearances is judged as part of their "artistic merit" score, and many judges do base at least part of their assessment on an athlete's weight. Also, skaters are always in pursuit of more rotations in their jumps, meaning that once they master a double axel (two and a half turns in the air), they immediately begin working on a triple axel (three and a half turns in the air). The next-to-impossible quadruple axel—the "quad," a breathtaking four and a half turns in the air—is every skater's dream, but only a handful can perform it. Jumps like these require the skater to literally defy gravity, which they reason is easier to do if they weigh less. Female pairs figure skaters have an extra challenge in this area: Their male partners must be able to lift them and hold them gracefully in midair. This meaning that the men must be strong but also that the women must be light.

So far little has been written about eating disorders in the world of figure skating, but the similarities between a skater's training routine and that of a dancer or gymnast cannot be ignored. Both male and female figure skaters are immersed in an environment that could be dangerous for an individual who is susceptible to developing an eating disorder.

Other Weight-Focused Sports

Other athletes who are required to control their weight for their sport include jockeys and lightweight football players. In a horse race, the jockey's job is, simply put, to get his or her horse to run faster than the rest. That job is harder when the horse is carrying a heavier load. For that reason, many jockeys are pressured, by themselves or others, to stay as light as they possibly can. This leads to some bizarre dynamics within the horse-racing culture, such as one jockey who bragged about his habit of eating just three peanuts for lunch. Since eating disorders can bring on premature osteoporosis in female victims, and since injuries, including broken bones, go with the territory of being a jockey, it follows that female jockeys suffering from eating disorders are in extreme danger.

A study published in 1994 revealed that 40 percent of lightweight football players showed signs of disordered eating. At the time that figure was the highest ever reported among male athletes. Of the 131 players studied, 42 percent had engaged in dysfunctional eating patterns, including bingeing and purging. Ten percent were identified as at risk for an eating disorder. In an article for *Science News*, Dr. Mary Turner DePalma told writer Susan S. Lang: "When athletes use unhealthful ways to quickly lose weight, such as techniques to achieve hypohydration (low body fluids), the athletes significantly increase their risk of injury and even fatality in a contact sport such as football."

Other Appearance-Focused Sports

Other athletes whose appearance is a factor in their success include cheerleaders, swimmers, and divers. Like dancers and pairs figure skaters, female cheerleaders' male partners must be able to lift them and hold them in the air. Often the girls balance with one foot on the hand of a male cheerleader. The sex-appeal factor of cheerleading also plays a significant role: In addition to having the skill to perform difficult moves and the cardiovascular fitness to endure one routine after another while yelling cheers, cheerleaders are supposed to be cute and perky, with pretty faces, perfect makeup and well-groomed hair, and nails.

Swimmers and divers, male and female, are also held to a high standard of appearance. Their swimsuits accentuate any fat deposits on the body, and they are judged at least partially by the appeal of their "line"—the way their bodies appear as they enter the water. A study of nearly 1,000 competitive swimmers ages nine to eighteen attending a summer training camp in 1985 revealed that 15.4 percent of the girls and 3.6 percent of the boys used unhealthy weight-loss techniques. "The swimmer's concerns about weight seemed to be more related to societal influences than to the demands of their sport," Dr. Gail M. Dummer and colleagues, the authors of the study, noted.

3

Building Up, Tearing Down

Athletes seem like walking advertisements for human perfection: fast, flexible, talented, toned, disciplined, motivated—they seem like people who could do anything if they put their minds to it. And that's part of the problem. Of course, the truth is that athletes, even superstars, are human just like the rest of us. But sometimes an athlete begins to believe that he or she really should be able to be, do, or control anything at all, including appetite, pain tolerance, and endurance. "They believe their single-minded discipline and ability to endure pain and injury set them apart and mark them as special people, even heroes, in a world gone comfortable and soft," the Web page of ANRED notes. "Elite athletes who have become addicted to exercise, and to the lifestyle that is admired in their sport's milieu, cannot see that they have fallen far from the goal of a healthy mind in a healthy body. They have become obsessive, compulsive, and vulnerable to permanent physical damage from minor injuries that they do not allow to heal by resting." One of the toughest things for an elite athlete to learn is that the body is breakable.

Another problem for athletes is that some people—parents, coaches, sponsors, judges—really do believe that the athlete should be able to do anything. When athletes are surrounded by people who continually drive them to try harder, do better, and ignore pain, hunger, and exhaustion, it's hard for those athletes to speak up for themselves, and it's hard for them to remember that every person has limits and pushing past them is not healthy. There is a difference between working to improve your performance and overtaxing your body to dangerous extremes, and athletes need people in their lives who will remind them of that fact and help them stay in balance.

Eating disorders are about control. The person suffering from an eating disorder feels a need to control his or her eating. There are many reasons why this situation can come up, but in athletes, two important factors are performance in the sport and societal expectations. Our society's demand that everyone be thin and fit affects all people, but some researchers argue that it impacts athletes even more. As the discussion of high-risk sports in the previous chapter showed, when combined with the desire to excel at a sport, these twin obsessions drive some athletes to diet and train literally to death.

THE ATHLETE'S WORLD

It got to where I never had anything to talk about with the few friends I had left outside of gymnastics. They got sick of hearing about my "hundred-and-one-falls," as they called it, and I didn't care about their boring stories of sitting around at different people's houses. We had nothing in common anymore.

Athletes' lives are in some ways similar to those of celebrities: They are isolated from "normal people," spending most of their time with others who do what they do. They are hyperfocused on their performance, and they are surrounded by a crew of nonathletes—coaches, trainers, parents, scouts, sponsors—who are also hyperfocused on their performance. Just as some celebrities often lose sight of what really matters in life, some athletes forget—indeed, they are often encouraged to ignore—aspects of life that conflict with or do not relate directly to the sport.

Many athletes are encouraged to do things that would be considered abnormal in nonathletes. They are praised for having the discipline to adhere to restrictive diets and excessive training, they are forgiven for neglecting friends and family, and they are expected to rise above common desires such as going to a party or having dessert if they are to succeed. Movies such as *Rocky* portray champions as people who cannot stop thinking about, dreaming about, or practicing to reach their goal. To put it in perspective, such single-mindedness and obsession are also trademark of another group of people: stalkers.

That's not to say that dedication and hours of hard work are something to be discouraged. But it is important to remember that everyone, even an

Olympic athlete, needs to have a life outside of sports. No one can continue to improve without rest, relaxation, and quality time with interesting people who have varying backgrounds. Research in the areas of time management and peak performance have shown that leaving the task and doing something else for a while, even if it's simply reading a book or taking a nap, will leave you mentally refreshed and will often spark creative thinking and problem solving and increase motivation. This downtime is doubly important in tasks involving physical exertion: Not only does the mind need an occasional rest, but the body does too.

Unfortunately, many athletes are not given the opportunity to take a break. They begin to feel like slaves to their sport, either because they are driven to overtrain by coaches or parents, or because they impose those restrictions on themselves, often in the belief that their diligence will pay off in improved performance or favored status with those coaches and parents. If the athlete is really good, he or she will likely be pressured even more and will not feel free to quit, unless someone influential and respected reinforces to the athletes value outside the sport. Many parents drive their children to continue in a sport long past the point where the child is interested in it. The reasons vary from practical ("You swore you

Movies such as *Rocky* portray champions as people who cannot stop thinking about, dreaming about, or practicing to reach their goal. To put it in perspective, such single-mindedness and obsession are also the trademark of another group of people: stalkers.

REVERSE ANOREXIA

There is a condition related to eating disorders that afflicts both male and female athletes. When a person has obvious, well-defined muscles but still believes he or she is too small, that person is suffering from a syndrome called muscle dysmorphia. Muscle dysmorphia is sometimes referred to as reverse anorexia because, instead of believing that they are too fat when they are actually thin, sufferers believe they are too small when in fact they may be dramatically muscu-lar. "Imagine a bodybuilder—250 pounds, 20-inch biceps, 6 percent body fat—horrified to take his shirt off for fear he looks out of shape," said Alicia Potter in the *Boston Phoenix*.

would keep skating if we bought you those $500 skates, so now we want you to keep your promise") to motivational ("You'll regret quitting now, and you'll wish we had pushed you") to abusive ("You have a chance to make a lot of money, and you owe it to us to repay us for everything we've done for you"). Feeling trapped and perceiving that his or her only value as a person is defined by performance in the sport, the athlete will do anything to continue to improve, including dangerous weight-cutting techniques and overtraining. Some truly desperate athletes try to injure themselves so they will have a legitimate reason to quit and will be able to do so with dignity.

YOU THINK YOU'RE IMPROVING YOUR BODY, BUT YOU'RE REALLY HURTING IT: THE PHYSICAL EFFECTS OF OVERTRAINING

You've already read about the physical effects of eating disorders in chapter one. In addition to all the damage a person can do to his or her body from anorexia, bulimia, or BED, overexercising can also cause serious, permanent injury. And if you don't care about the consequences as long as you're a champion, note this: It is possible to train so much that you actually hurt your performance. ANRED notes: "Cardiovascular health requires that 2,000 to 3,500 calories be burned each week in aerobic exercise: running, jogging, dancing, brisk walking, and so forth . . . After 3,500 hundred calories are burned per week, the health benefits decrease, and the risk of injury increases." Overdoing strength training can also be detrimental: "Overdoing weight-bearing exercise can tear down muscle tissue instead of building it, and also damage bones, joints, cartilage, tendons, and ligaments."

As overtraining continues, injuries such as stress fractures begin to plague the athlete. The athlete will be unwilling to slow down and allow injuries to heal, however, seeing them as a sign of weakness and feeling therefore even more desperate to continue training. Some athletes will begin to turn to performance-enhancing drugs and painkillers to keep going. "If the exercise addict abuses steroid drugs in an effort to increase muscle mass," ANRED notes, "s/he faces additional risks: blurred vision, hallucinations, rages and tantrums, depression, acne, other skin problems, increased blood pressure, muscle cramps, joint pain, loss of sex drive, and mood swings."

A DANGEROUS COMBINATION: YOUNG WOMEN AND THE FEMALE ATHLETE TRIAD

Yet another risk to eating-disordered female athletes is a set of conditions known as the Female Athlete Triad. Consisting of amenorrhea, disordered eating, and osteoporosis, the condition is extremely dangerous, potentially fatal—and alarmingly common. While an estimated 1 percent of the female population is considered anorexic and another 2 to 3 percent are bulimic, various studies have found that anywhere from 15 to 70 percent of female athletes practice pathogenic, or disease-causing, weight-control behaviors, which in some cases include anorexia and/or bulimia. Nattiv and Lynch emphasized in their essay in *The Physician and Sportsmedicine,* "Although they may not fit the . . . criteria for anorexia or bulimia, they are still at risk for developing serious psychiatric, endocrine, and skeletal problems."

Approximately 2 to 5 percent of women in the general population have amenorrhea, but its prevalence among female athletes is estimated at anywhere from 3.4 percent to 66 percent, depending on the study's definition of the condition and the characteristics of its subject group. Although there are many possible causes for amenorrhea (including the most obvious, pregnancy), in a female athlete the condition should alert the young woman's doctor or coach to evaluate her closely for disordered eating and osteoporosis. Even if the other elements of the triad can be ruled out, amenorrhea should not be considered "normal" and allowed to continue without a thorough search for its cause. Although it once was believed that simply dipping below a certain percentage of body fat could cause an otherwise fit and healthy young woman's periods to stop, and was therefore not serious, further research has begun to show that the situation is not that simple. It is important to understand that amenorrhea is not healthy, even though the young woman experiencing it may welcome the convenience of not having a period each month and may even believe, falsely, that losing her period is a point of pride and indicates overall fitness.

Most people who hear the term "osteoporosis" think of very old women with hunched backs, weak joints, and bones that break with just one fall. Most young women do not consider themselves at risk for the condition, and in fact it is not common for a normal woman to develop it in her younger years. However, the combination of disordered eating and amenorrhea puts a young woman, even a teenager or woman in her twenties, at serious risk for loss of bone density. This loss is presently believed to be irreversible. This means that the woman's skeleton, which may not have finished growing, will never again be as strong as it was before the condition set in. She will be prone to stress fractures and other breaks that aren't caused by an accident or fall. Far from being a strong athlete, she will be left permanently fragile and severely limited in the activities in which she can participate.

As Loren Mooney reported in *Cornell Magazine,* "Some athletes trim down to a light, but natural, competition weight and improve their performance. Others can cross the fine line to become compulsive about weight loss." The key is finding an ideal weight for performance and health; this is something most adolescents are ill-equipped to do on their own, and it's the reason a well-informed, attentive coach who demonstrates healthy priorities for his or her team is crucial to every athlete's success and well-being. The emphasis should always be on maintaining overall wellness; if there is even the slightest possibility that reducing body-fat percentage may be unhealthy for an athlete, it should be discouraged. The bottom line? Work hard to reach your goals, but never risk your health to be number one.

DOES YOUR COACH KNOW WHAT'S GOOD FOR YOU?

Some coaches do, and some don't. L. W. Rosen and colleagues made that point in an article for the journal *The Physician and Sportsmedicine:* "Although little controlled research addresses the issue of optimum weight/height ratios for peak performance, most coaches and trainers establish weight goals for their athletes. Yet survey data on coaches in a major athletic conference revealed that coaches know very little about nutrition as it relates to athletic performance."

If your coach pressures you to lose weight in unhealthy ways, don't go along with him or her. Show your coach this book and point out that you believe it would be unhealthy for you to weigh any less than you do now. If your coach won't listen to you, don't just drop the subject. Switch to another sport, or, if you really love the one you're in, talk to another coach, your parents, or a counselor about ways you can continue to participate in your sport while resisting the coach's bad advice. Remember that your coach probably does not intend to hurt you, but is fixated on winning and needs to learn about the dire consequences of disordered eating and unhealthy weight loss. Speaking up for yourself will keep you safe and may prevent that coach from harming other athletes as well.

WHAT'S ON YOUR MIND?
THE PSYCHOLOGICAL COMPONENT
OF DISORDERED EATING AND EXERCISE
COMPULSION

While the specific reasons that a person develops an eating disorder are unique to that individual, there are a number of factors that are believed to be common triggers and may be shared by many sufferers, athletes and nonathletes, regardless of age, gender, ethnicity, or social class.

In her book *Good Enough: When Losing Is Winning, Perfection Becomes Obsession, and Thin Enough Can Never Be Achieved,* Cynthia N. Bitter describes how it feels for an anorexic to look at herself in a mirror:

> I turned on the light in the tiny hospital bathroom, walked over to the sink and looked down into the white porcelain basin, too afraid to look in the mirror. Too afraid to see what I had done . . . of my own free will. I raised my eyes, slowly, and stared into my face. Oh God, my face! Gaunt, sunken-in eyes. Hollow cheeks; scrawny chicken-neck. Parched yellowish skin that called out for hydration, for nutrition . . . for food. How had this happened? What monster had I become? Okay, I'm scared. I'm scared because it's not getting any better. This merry-go-round won't slow down, or let me get off. I wish I could go back to the beginning and start over. But I can't. And I can't stop. Not until I'm thin. Not until my

breastbone rests on my backbone, will I be assured that all is safe . . . that I am thin.

Although it is true that victims of eating disorders are obsessed with thinness, to say, as some people do, that they are therefore vain and self-centered is insensitive and ignorant. Eating disorder sufferers may seem to want to be thinner and, in the case of athletes, more skilled than everyone else, but what they really want is to be accepted. They focus on losing weight because they believe that they will never be worthy of love unless they are thin. This fear is unfounded to begin with because the people who truly love you don't base that love on your appearance or performance in a sport. But to make matters even worse, eating disorder sufferers, especially anorexics, lose the ability to know what "thin" really is, eventually reaching a point where they see themselves as fat when everyone else who looks at them sees sharply defined cheekbones, elbows, knees, ribs and collarbones, and sometimes the outline of internal organs showing through the skin.

So, not only are eating disorder sufferers chasing an ideal that won't bring them happiness, but that ideal is continually dropping to ever more unattainable levels. For them, there will always be "just five more pounds."

HOW DOES IT START?

I think mine started when my mother saw me in my new softball uniform. She hardly even said anything; she just looked at my hips in the tight pants, got this look of concern on her face, and just said, "Hmm." I can't remember being too concerned about my hips before then, but after that it was all I thought about. I always wore my uniform shirt untucked to cover my hips and butt.

Eating disorders can be triggered by anything, or by a combination of factors. It is common for them to set in at a stressful time in the victim's life, such as puberty, a breakup, changing schools, or dealing with family problems. The beginning of an eating disorder can be compared to a tornado: In order for it to start, a number of conditions must come together in the right combination and at the right time. Once those conditions are there, some sort of storm is inevitable.

Eating disorders often start as a diet, but soon the victim finds that he or she can't stop dieting and working out, even after reaching the original goal. The American Anorexia/Bulimia Association points out, "It is worth remembering that an eating disorder is not only a problem but also an attempted solution to a problem. That is, the disorder serves some purpose. Like many other symptoms and apparently maladaptive behaviors, an eating disorder, for all of the problems it creates, is an effort to cope and to communicate." In the case of the eating-disordered athlete, the problem is often hidden behind what looks like a noble attempt to improve performance.

Some researchers are investigating a possible link between eating disorders and brain chemistry. The National Institute of Mental Health has reported that people with anorexia and certain forms of depression tend to have higher-than-normal levels of cortisol, a hormone released in the brain during times of stress. This excess production of cortisol has been linked to a problem in or near the region of the brain known as the hypothalamus. Another hormone, vasopressin, has also been found in high concentrations in people with eating disorders and is believed to contribute to obsessive behavior such as that seen in anorexics and suffers of obsessive-compulsive disorder.

PRESSURE TO PERFORM: YOUR RELATIONSHIP WITH YOUR COACH AND TEAM

Athletes have some special challenges to face when dealing with an eating disorder because often the sport in which they participate has become part of the problem. It may be the reason that the eating disorder developed—a desperate attempt to improve performance—or the person may simply have been drawn to the sport as an outlet for his or her exercise compulsion. Either way, once you have recognized that you have a problem and decide that you want to do something about it, you will need the support of everyone close to you, including those you know through your sport.

If you are a young athlete, chances are you have a coach, or perhaps even more than one. It is also likely that you are a member of a team of other athletes who count on you to help them win. These relationships are often among the richest and most rewarding of a young person's life, but they can also be harmful to an eating-disordered athlete. The reaction you get from coaches and teammates when you tell them about your problem and your need to change your training routine will play a big part in your recovery. So how can you keep the obligation you feel to your coach and your team from interfering with your health?

First, you should understand just how influential a coach can be to a young athlete. In many cases, coaches become like second parents to their team, and the athletes respond with an undying desire to make the coach proud of them. It doesn't even matter whether the athlete and coach like each other. If they do, the athlete will want to please the coach and earn his or her praise, but if not, the athlete will adopt an "I'll show you" attitude and work harder to avoid the coach's disdain. This bond can bring out the best in athletes, helping them to reach for goals and use every bit of ability and energy they can find. But there is a potentially dangerous element to the desire to please the coach. Since the relationship between an athlete and a coach is based on the learning of a sport, the single most important way in which the athlete can gain the coach's favor is by excelling in the sport. While many coaches praise and even insist upon other achievements such as good grades or community service, it is understood that the primary reason for their relationship is the sport. Therefore, if an athlete is not especially good at the sport or doesn't seem to care as much about it or try as hard as others, he or she simply won't receive as much positive feedback from the coach as others will.

In their report to the President's Council on Physical Fitness and Sports, entitled "Physical Activity and Sport in the Lives of Girls," Patty

Freedson and Linda Bunker asserted, "It should be noted that the presence of disordered eating is not only seen in elite-level athletes but also among young girls who strive to be elite-level performers. Young athletes who are not particularly successful in sport may also be susceptible to this problem as they see their dietary practices as something they can control and use to please their coach or parent despite the fact that high-level performance is not possible."

Once you understand how strong of an influence your coach's view of you may be having on your opinion of yourself, you can begin to look at how that relationship may affect your recovery. Think hard about your coach's attitude, and be honest with yourself. Does he berate people who fall behind in drills or who don't perform as well as the rest of the team? Does she publicly criticize anyone's weight or appearance? Does he get angry or seem to take it personally if someone's performance doesn't measure up to his standards? Does she remind you of a drill sergeant? No matter how much you may respect your coach, if he or she seems to believe in winning at any cost, you may not get the support you need to heal. A coach with misplaced priorities may consider your eating disorder a sign of weakness and may treat you like a quitter or a burden with which he or she does not want to be bothered. Some coaches even ignore the signs of eating disorders completely, insisting that dieting, weight cutting, and overtraining are the price to be paid for becoming a champion. These are worst-case scenarios, but unfortunately they do happen. Coaches are human and, like people from every other walk of life, there are good ones and bad ones. It is critical that you separate the coach's ability in the sport—his or her win/loss record—from his or her reliability as a mentor to you. It may be true that your coach produces more champions than anyone else, but at what price?

If you determine that your coach will not be supportive if you tell him or her about your problem, then you will have to find other people to help you, such as parents, teachers, guidance counselors, friends, and your doctor. If you believe your coach, and by extension your team, will be supportive, then you have one more critic to overcome: yourself.

In order to recover from your eating disorder, you must recognize the enormous pressure you put on yourself, in your sport and in the rest of your life. Even if you believe that your coach and teammates will want to help you regain your health, you may still feel as if you are letting them down. Recognize your need to please your coach and your team, to be a hero or a star or the champion in your sport. In the end, the only person whose opinion of you matters is you; as an athlete, you may need to spend some time learning to separate your performance in your sport from your self-worth and value as a person.

There is an even bigger psychological obstacle at work here, and it is one that all eating disorder sufferers face, but among athletes it is especially pronounced. That obstacle is our society's belief in putting aside personal needs for the good of the team, or the company, or the family, or the country, or any other worthy cause. When gymnast Kerri Strug landed a vault with an injured ankle in the

1996 Olympics, she became a hero for putting her team before herself. Such "team spirit" is considered admirable—it got Strug the Olympic Spirit Award and her picture on a Wheaties box, along with her team gold medal—but it isn't good to sacrifice your health in order to win. This isn't war, after all—it's just a game. If you can take this philosophy to heart and stop putting "bigger causes" ahead of your most important personal needs, you will have taken an important step toward recovery.

PRESSURE TO CONFORM: HOW SOCIETY'S DEMANDS AFFECT YOU

Research has shown that the pressures exerted by society are among the most important factors affecting a young person's self-esteem. Unfortunately, what society says can have an unhealthy impact. While traditionally, girls have felt more of a negative impact than boys, society has begun to impose unrealistic ideals on males as well. You are probably not aware of how great an influence society's "rules" may have on you. Ask yourself:

⊙ Do I feel that I must wear cosmetics to cover up pimples, scars, or variations in my skin tone so that my skin will appear "flawless"?

⊙ Do I refuse to leave the house unless my hair and nails are perfect?

⊙ When someone pays me a compliment, do I believe them?

⊙ What prompts me to want to buy or wear a certain article of clothing? Is it comfort, or is it because other kids I admire are wearing it? Is it to cover up parts of my body that I don't want anyone to notice?

⊙ Do I refuse to go swimming because I wouldn't be caught dead in a bathing suit in front of anyone else? Do I avoid certain sports or part-time jobs because of the uniforms?

⊙ Do I have rules for buying clothes, such as "no stripes" or "only dark colors," that I believe enhance my body?

⊙ Would I exercise as much as I do now if appearance did not matter in our society?

⊙ Do I suck in my stomach when someone I consider attractive walks by?

⊙ Do I feel uncomfortable eating in front of others, even if I feel hungry? Does it depend on whether the food is "good" or "bad"?

Think about your answers to these questions. If your answers show that you wish you could hide your body from other people or that you deny yourself fun experiences because you are afraid you're not good-looking enough, then you are struggling under the weight of society's expectations of you.

HOW SOCIETY'S "RULES" ARE CONVEYED TO US: THE MEDIA

"The media" refers to all of the print, radio, and television news organizations in our country, and by extension the entertainment industry. It is very unfortunate that journalism and entertainment have merged to such an unhealthy extent because journalism, in its purest form, is supposed to be an unbiased, neutral presentation of the facts of a story. As news organizations began to recognize the value of advertising to finance their operations, they became more and more dependent upon it, and soon the line between simply reporting the news and reporting it in a way that made their advertisers look good began to blur. Now it's sometimes hard to tell whether you're watching a news program or a paid advertisement. Companies with something to sell often buy full-page ads in newspapers and magazines that look just like a news story or feature article. Few sporting events would happen without sponsors, companies that pay to have their logo prominently displayed in the arena or worn by the players. The most blatant example of this is auto racing, where drivers are coached to wear caps with their sponsor's logo and find a way to say the sponsor's name every time a camera and microphone are put in front of them. Such promotional tactics are also common in movies: When an actor takes a drink of Coke or Pepsi in a movie, it's not because the character prefers it—it's because Coke or Pepsi paid for the right to have their logo displayed in that film.

All of this is not inherently bad, but it is incredibly manipulative. Many worthwhile causes would get little attention without corporate sponsorship or the sale of advertising space, but the help comes with strings attached: when you have a sponsor, you are expected to help your sponsor gain new customers.

The important thing to know as a consumer in American society—and you became a consumer the very first time you asked your parents to buy you something—is the motivation behind all the commercials, magazine and newspaper ads, and prominent displays of brand-name items that you see every day. Companies don't really know what is best for you, and they don't know how to make you popular, witty, or pretty; they can't make your life trouble-free. But they want you to think that that's what buying their products will do for you! Their goal is to make money. They make money when you buy something of theirs. Therefore, they want you to buy their stuff, whether you need it or not. Some companies don't care that their products could injure you or make you sick—they just want your money. This is what the recent controversy over cigarette companies is all about. In most cases, however, advertisers justify their hard-sell methods with the assertion that buying and using something you don't need won't actually harm you. Other than the bite it takes out of your savings, buying these products might seem harmless. But is it?

PRESSURE FROM WITHIN: HOW YOUR SELF-IMAGE RUNS YOUR LIFE

If you could do only one thing to avoid problems with disordered eating, what would it be? What do you

THE MOCKING OF ANOREXIA

An editorial in *Glamour* magazine's February 1999 issue addressed the "tabloid trend of diagnosing skinny celebrities as sick." The issue became more prominent around that time when Calista Flockhart, star of the popular TV series *Ally McBeal,* was seen at the Emmy Awards in a gown that revealed much of her extremely thin frame. Catty tabloid articles and jokes began to fly, along with rumors and accusations that Flockhart was anorexic. The *Glamour* writer asked, "Why did her weight loss inspire jokes and gossip, not concern? Would the rumors have been as mean spirited if she'd been diagnosed with, say, breast cancer?"

"Anorexia has become a joke of a disease," the writer continued. "We use the term to describe any woman who's skinny—whether she's perfectly healthy or possibly sick—and in doing so, we trivialize an illness that is excruciatingly real."

Such mocking can be devastating to true victims of anorexia or other eating disorders, who may feel that they will be laughed at or ridiculed if their condition becomes public knowledge. The *Glamour* writer noted one Florida psychologist's experience with a patient who was extremely upset by a TV interview with a group of models who made a joke of sharing a single strawberry for breakfast. "My patient felt as if the terrible disease she has is a joke to the rest of the world," the psychologist said. "But an eating disorder is an agonizing illness—that fact really is minimized."

think is the single most important factor in preventing anorexia, bulimia, and other eating disorders?

Although there are always many reasons behind each person's eating disorder, the one element that could make the most difference is building self-esteem. This is increasingly difficult for people in our society to do.

In fact, some people are never able to do it, and they go through life basing their opinion of themselves on their weight or muscularity or skin tone or hair color or any other thing about their bodies that they think others will judge them on. Instead of concentrating on being a better person on the inside, these people feel that they must spend lots of time, effort, and money on what they are on the outside in order to be loved. The saddest thing about that is that it's a losing battle: Everyone's body ages and changes, so even if by some miracle you do manage to achieve the physical perfection you've always dreamed of, it won't last. What does last is the work you do to become a wiser, kinder, more generous, more caring person, and once you begin to excel in those areas, you will attract people who are also interested in being wiser, kinder, more generous, and more caring—in other words, you will become more lovable, and so you will be loved even more.

Yeah, but that's not so easy to believe when you have a huge pimple on your nose and your jeans don't fit and the prom is a week away and you're dateless, right? The trick is to break out of thinking from day to day, moment to moment, crisis to crisis, and instead focus on long-term goals. Once you know what you want in life, you can begin to work toward it over time, and things like a bad hair day or a dateless weekend won't seem so important anymore. Why? Because you have bigger, more important things to look forward to.

But what if you don't know what you want to do with your life? No problem. Having a strong sense of self-worth doesn't mean you have to have your life all planned out. Most high school students don't really know what they want to do with their lives, even though they are experiencing tremendous pressure to commit to something—some career or college or the military or religious life or marriage and kids. Not knowing what you want but feeling pressured to figure it out quickly can be so stressful that it can affect your self-esteem.

The truth is that you can have long-term goals

THE POWER OF SELF-TALK

People who study self-esteem emphasize the value of positive self-talk. Self-talk refers to the statements you make to yourself, or about yourself to others, regarding your behavior, your performance at some task, your looks, your worth, or any other thing about you. You might not even be aware of doing it, but try to listen to your self-talk. Is it negative or positive? Just about everyone has told themselves they're stupid at one time or another; that is an example of negative self-talk. Learning to stop negative self-talk and teaching yourself to use positive self-talk is one good way to improve your self-esteem. From now on, work on stopping yourself from saying or thinking things like "I'm so stupid!" or "Why would anyone want to go out with me?" or "I'll never be able to do this." Instead, learn to be kind and patient with yourself. Tell yourself things like "I'm not stupid, I just don't get this yet" or "If he (or she) doesn't think I'm good enough for him (or her), then he (or she) is obviously not good enough for me" or "I know I can do this if I just keep trying." Praising and encouraging yourself is not arrogant or con-ceited, and although it may seem cutesy at first, it's a healthy way to raise your self-esteem, and that will help you be the type of person you want to be.

for yourself that don't require the selection of any one path—not yet. First, figure out what your values are, decide what type of person you want to be, and begin working toward becoming that person. Everything you learn about yourself as you develop your own personal moral code will help you choose a life that will make you happy.

For athletes who have spent years in pursuit of excellence in their sport, thinking about life goals is especially important. Too often, an athlete will work toward a championship, only to come away from that competition with no idea of what should come next. This is true whether the athlete won the gold or didn't even place in the runners-up. The single-mindedness that got that athlete as far as a championship competition also prevented him or her from thinking about what to do with his or her life afterwards. High school athletes may follow their sport into college with a scholarship, but the vast majority of college athletes do not go on to the pros, so their athletic careers end with graduation. Having no idea what path to take and feeling desperately lost, many now-former athletes make poor choices in haste, entering whatever career seems most available or perhaps marrying and starting a family before they're ready because it seems like "the thing to do."

If you are an athlete, make sure that your self-esteem is based on something more than your athletic prowess. Work on improving yourself in other ways, including as a friend, and devise realistic, non-sports-related goals for your life so you'll have others things on which to base your opinion of yourself. Then, if you don't do as well as you would like in your sport, or if you choose to quit or are forced to by an injury, your entire self-image won't be destroyed.

MAYBE IT'S SOMETHING ELSE: RELATED CONDITIONS

There are a number of conditions that often occur along with eating disorders or that may be mistaken for eating disorders. Several of them are described below. If you suspect that you may have any of these conditions, or if you see signs in a friend, please seek help. The section entitled Where to Go for Help at the end of this book contains many helpful resources.

Malnutrition

Kyle: "I hate vegetables, and I don't really like fruit either. Everything I like comes out of a can or a bottle or a drive-through window. My parents try to eat healthy, but I don't like any of the stuff they make, and I can tell they don't really like it either—they just eat it because it's supposedly good for them and to set a good example for us kids. It doesn't work, though—I just eat what I want."

Most people think of malnutrition as a chronic condition affecting only poverty-stricken children in other countries, where there isn't enough food, and water for everyone. Malnutrition exists in America, even among people who can have all the food they want. In cases of child abuse and neglect, it is not uncommon to find that the victims have not been fed properly; they may be low on certain vitamins and minerals or they may be so starved that their bellies are swollen like those of the children in the pictures we all see from impoverished countries. However, many children with loving parents are lacking in vitamins and minerals crucial for health and growth, including calcium and iron. The reason for this is poor eating habits.

A child who always drinks pop instead of milk will almost certainly develop a calcium deficiency. A child, especially a girl, who is allowed to eat no red meat but is not taught how to get the iron she needs from other food sources may become anemic. These are common, completely preventable forms of malnutrition in this country. Among older children and even adults, fad dieting can also lead to malnutrition. Any diet that severely limits or forbids the consumption of an entire food group, such as carbohydrates or fats, puts the dieter in danger of missing out on important nutrients, either because they are found mostly in the forbidden foods, or because they come from allowable foods but cannot be absorbed by the body without the help of the forbidden foods.

Besides depriving your body of important nutrients, which in some cases cannot be replaced simply by taking a daily multivitamin, limiting yourself to a strict diet regimen that does not include any of your favorite foods can backfire. The lack of certain foods, such as fats, combined with the psychological strain of harsh dieting, can bring on a binge in which you "lose control" and eat everything you've been forcing yourself to avoid. The subsequent guilt that you feel after the binge then prompts you to go back on the same, or an even stricter, diet. This cycle of impossible dieting and loss of control is called yo-yo dieting, and it is bad for your health; besides putting you at risk for malnutrition, it could lead to an eating disorder.

It is important that every child learn about the body's nutritional requirements and think about them with every meal and snack. A child who understands that drinking pop, eating candy, skipping meals, or avoiding entire food groups all the time is damaging to his or her health will be more likely to make better choices. If you recognize these or similar poor eating habits in yourself, do some research on nutrition and begin to make healthy changes in the way you eat. If you don't get well-balanced meals at home, list some healthy meals and foods and ask the person who prepares your meals to make them for you. It is never too late to learn about nutrition and to begin to provide your body with the proper fuel.

Smoking and Substance Abuse

Kylie: "My parents really gave me a hard time when they first caught me smoking. I knew they would, but I figure they've got no right to talk because they both smoke like chimneys."

Tim: "My parents make a big show out of trying to control me, but I end up doing what I want. Like if we go to a wedding together and it has an open bar, first they tell me I can't drink. Then, when I come back with a beer, they act all stern and say, 'Well, just one.' Then they act like they don't notice when I get a shot of tequila. They just don't want to look like they can't control me, but they know I'm going to do what I

IS IT HEALTHY TO BE A VEGETARIAN?

There is one diet variation that eliminates food categories but can be followed in a healthy manner: vegetarianism. Traditionally, being a vegetarian has meant not eating meat, but there are actually quite a number of variations on vegetarianism. Some people simply do not eat beef or other red meats; others avoid all animal products, including beef, chicken, pork, fish, eggs, and dairy products such as milk, cheese, and yogurt; and many people's vegetarian habits fall somewhere between these two extremes. A person's reasons for choosing a vegetarian diet may include religious or political beliefs that forbid eating another creature, or health considerations linked to allergies or animal fats. If you are a vegetarian, it is possible for you to fulfill your nutritional needs, but it takes much more planning and effort and may be more expensive. If you choose a vegetarian lifestyle, make sure you educate yourself and are committed to it for healthy reasons, not for weight loss or because your friends are doing it.

want, so they find ways to make it look like they're letting me do it but on their terms."

Lyssa: "I started smoking pot when I first ran away. I was brought back, and my parents cried and said they would try to do better with me, but things didn't really change. It's easier to tolerate now, though, because I can just get high and forget about it."

Any foreign substance that you put into your body alters it in some way. Tobacco, alcohol, and all drugs and supplements have various effects on your brain, heart, lungs, kidneys, liver, or other organs, and also on your body's respiratory, circulatory, endocrine, and digestive systems. Medications are used to make you better if you're sick by bringing on good changes in your body's organs and systems. Supplements are intended to help your body reach its highest health potential. You have probably heard about the negative effects that smoking, drinking, and using drugs can have on your body, but did you know that they can also contribute to disordered eating?

Many people believe that smoking can make you lose weight, so many girls use cigarettes as a dieting tool. This is extremely dangerous to your health, and it doesn't even work! The reason some people lose weight when they start smoking is that they tend to replace snacks with cigarettes. The reason some people gain weight when they quit smoking is just the opposite: Instead of "consuming" a cigarette, they reach for a snack. If you teach yourself to find something else to do with your hands and mouth instead of smoking or overeating, for example, a hobby such as singing or drawing, or get involved in an activity that you can't do while smoking or eating, such as a sport, you can avoid two health risks, smoking and overeating, at the same time.

Drinking alcohol lowers your inhibitions and your ability to make good choices. Alcoholic beverages contain many calories on their own, and when people drink they also tend to eat more than normal. So, besides being dangerous to your health and your safety, not to mention illegal if you're underage, drinking can lead to binge eating. Drinking can also lead to malnutrition if it becomes the chronic condition known as *alcoholism*.

Many drugs have some of the same effects as alcohol: They lower your inhibitions, make you feel superconfident or invincible, or make you forget all the reasons you have for trying to eat healthy foods. Some drugs also increase or decrease your appetite. Laxatives, which are supposed to be used when you are constipated, and diuretics, which force your body to rid itself of water, are both commonly abused by people with eating disorders. Syrup of ipecac, which is intended to be used only to induce vomiting in people who have ingested poisons, is a poison itself and can cause death when misused. The use of any drug for a purpose other than the one listed on the label can be extremely dangerous. No drug should be used to lose weight or to purge excess calories. The only exception to this rule is the use of a prescription drug, prescribed to you (not to a friend or parent) by a doctor and to be used under that doctor's close supervision. Even then, drug use should be a last resort for treating a dangerously obese person; a good, responsible doctor will never prescribe a weight-loss drug to a child or teen who simply wants to look better.

Of course, in many cases the use of tobacco, alcohol, or drugs points to a problem more severe than disordered eating. If you are currently using any of these substances, please stop trying to convince yourself that you can handle it, that it's no big deal, that everyone is doing it, or that it won't hurt you. The truth is that it is a big deal and it will hurt you, and possibly kill you. Please find someone who can help you stop. There are groups listed in the Where to Go for Help section at the end of this book that exist to help with any problem, not just eating disorders.

Depression

Alan: "I think maybe I'm depressed. My parents keep telling me I am. But what's the use of that? It's like telling someone they're ugly—like they can do anything about it."

Most people who suffer from eating disorders are also suffering to some degree from depression. Defined as an emotional condition characterized by feelings of hopelessness, inadequacy, or self-hatred, depression can be caused by any number of things or by nothing specific. Some people are prone to depression because of a chemical imbalance in their brains, but other people become depressed as a result of a crisis or sad occurrence in their lives or because they feel unable to cope with everyday life. Depression does not cause eating disorders, and eating disorders do not cause depression; instead, the circumstances in a person's life that cause one con-dition can also cause the other. When they occur together, both conditions must be treated in order to bring the sufferer back to a healthy, functional state. The health professional treating a victim of an eating disorder, or depression, or both, may prescribe an antidepressant medication to assist the sufferer in regaining psychological control and equilibrium. When that is accomplished, the person is better able to learn what she needs to change in her life to bring about recovery. It is important to realize that an antidepressant is not a cure; it simply reduces or eliminates the symptoms of depression and allows the sufferer to work on changing the things that brought it on in the first place.

Self-Mutilation

> *Evie: "Sometimes it just gets to be too much and the only thing that makes me feel better is cut-ting myself. I take my time with it so it will last. Sometimes I pull out my eyelashes, too, and I've also pulled out clumps of my hair. I haven't been able to do that last one lately, though—none of it is long enough to reach my mouth anymore."*

Some people act on their feelings of self-hatred by actually injuring themselves. But unlike the anorexic, who injures his or her body by depriving it of nutrients and straining its organs and systems, people who practice self-mutilation cut their bodies with a knife or razor blade, burn themselves, pull out their hair, eyelashes, or eyebrows, or do something else to cause themselves pain. They do not con-sciously intend to commit suicide; instead, their goal is to replace their emotional pain with more tolerable physical pain, to break through their emotional numbness and allow themselves to feel something, or to express anger or other painful feelings.

People who practice self-mutilation are also often suffering from an eating disorder. The thing that self-mutilators have in common with anorexics, bulimics, binge eaters, alcoholics, and drug abusers is that they are attempting to rid themselves of psychological pain.

Obsessive-Compulsive Disorder

Lanita: "I go to bed before my mom, but I can't go to sleep until I hear her go into her room. Then I get up and check the locks on all the doors and windows, and I make sure the alarm is set. Sometimes I can sleep after that, but sometimes I lie awake worrying about the windows in her room because I can't check those. And if I hear a noise, I have to go do it all over again or I will just lose my mind worrying."

Obsessive-compulsive disorder, or OCD, is a serious psychological condition characterized by rigid adherence to rituals such as checking door locks ten times each night, or washing your hands after touching anything or anyone (sometimes dozens of times each day). Jack Nicholson's character in the movie *As Good as It Gets* suffered from OCD, and he had rituals for locking doors, putting on his shoes, washing his hands, avoiding sidewalk cracks, and many other common elements of daily life. When he was forced to deviate from these rituals, he experienced great psychological distress—fear, confusion, and desperation to return his life to "normal."

Rituals are also common among eating disorder sufferers. Something as simple as refusing to eat any food that has touched another food on your plate, or insisting on eating one food at a time in a particular order (for example, the potatoes first, then the meat, then the vegetable) may signal an unhealthy preoccupation with eating. Such rituals do not automatically indicate that the person who follows them is suffering from OCD, but it could mean that the person has an underlying problem that is causing him or her to seek comfort in rigidly prescribed routines.

"I'm Running and I Can't Stop": How to Find Help

If you believe that you have a problem with compulsive exercise or an eating disorder, or if you suspect that a friend, teammate, or family member does, it is critically important to get help right away. Studies have shown that those who receive early treatment have a better chance for a full recovery than those whose condition persists for years. Left untreated, eating disorders can have irreversible consequences and can even be fatal.

If you are anorexic or bulimic, you may feel that your control of your eating is the only comforting thing in your life. Understandably, you may be afraid to give it up. But please know that when you give up your eating disorder, you will replace it with many other comforting, healthy things that will bring you happiness, not illness.

Of all the forms of disordered eating, anorexia is often the most difficult to treat because the victim often does not want to change. Anorexia is an emotional illness, and it alters your thinking in many ways. Anorexics believe that being thin is the most

74

HOW CAN I TELL
IF I HAVE AN EATING DISORDER
OR EXERCISE COMPULSION?

Ask yourself:

⊙ Do I think about food a lot, even when I'm not hungry?

⊙ Do I prefer eating alone?

⊙ Do I count every calorie I consume, even in chewing gum? Do I meticulously inspect and examine my food for any signs that something is wrong with it?

⊙ Am I happy with myself?

⊙ Do I diet frequently?

⊙ Do I ever fast or avoid eating for an entire day or more?

⊙ Have I ever used laxatives or diuretics (water pills) in an attempt to lose weight?

⊙ Do I ever "lose control" and eat a much larger than normal amount of food at one time?

⊙ Do I have irregular periods, or none at all?

⊙ Do I force myself to stick to a strict exercise regimen and feel like a loser if I miss a workout?

⊙ Have I ever made myself throw up after eating?

⊙ Do I believe that being in control of my eating shows others that I am in control of my life?

⊙ Do I feel pressured to get above-average grades and excel at every sport and hobby that I try?

⊙ Do I lie about what I eat?

⊙ Do I feel like I would rather die than be fat?

If any of these questions have raised a red flag in your mind, consider talking to a parent, counselor, teacher, coach, or other trusted adult to further explore the possibility that you are suffering from disordered eating.

important thing in their lives, and they see others' attempts to help them as a betrayal or sabotage of their efforts. Many anorexics do not want to stop, even when they see the damage they are doing to their bodies; others do want to stop but are afraid because anorexia has become the biggest part of their existence and they are afraid that without it they will be nothing.

CAN I FIX THIS MYSELF?

If you believe that you suffer from disordered eating or recognize the symptoms of an eating disorder in yourself, you've taken the most important step in helping yourself: You've identified the problem. Reading this book has given you a lot of information on your condition, including the dangerous consequences you will face if you don't find a way to stop it, and it has also given you much food for thought as to the reasons that you might have developed this problem. You can find many more books to read in the For Further Reading section at the end of this book; some of these sources might offer information more closely tailored to your individual situation.

If you believe that you are at risk for developing an eating disorder but don't have one yet, educating yourself may be all you need. Read everything you can find about disordered eating, and learn as much as you can about good nutrition and healthy, moderate exercise. Then make positive changes in your eating habits and your workout routine. Remember that your self-esteem and body image are very important to your well-being; practice positive self-talk on a regular basis, and surround yourself with positive people who make you feel good about your-self. Speak out against unrealistic media images, and refuse to participate in "body bashing," even if all the popular kids are doing it. Always remember that you are a lovable, worthwhile person no matter what you look like, and anyone who values you only for your looks or your performance in sports is not good for you. Celebrate your unique qualities, and encourage your friends to do the same for themselves. You can be a positive force in other people's lives as well.

Do you recall the distinction between disordered eating and eating disorders that was explained in the first chapter? Although it is possible to correct disordered eating on your own, helping yourself recover from an eating disorder be extremely diffi-cult—if not impossible—without professional help. Even if you are able to force yourself to eat, to resist bingeing and purging, or to keep from overexercis-ing, no amount of willpower can erase the emo-tional issues that led you to seek comfort in those behaviors. If you feel that you might need more help than you can find in books but you aren't ready to talk about it yet, it's okay to wait until you've thor-oughly researched your problem and sorted out for yourself how you want to go about changing it before you tell your parents or ask another trusted adult for help, *as long as you aren't in immediate danger.* If you are experiencing any disturbing phys-ical symptoms, such as an irregular heartbeat, bleeding, fainting or dizzy spells, or pain, don't wait—tell someone and make it clear that you need immediate help.

In any case, don't take too long to seek help. Make a commitment to yourself to ask for help two weeks from today, and use that time to finish this book and check out others at the library, and to think through how you want to handle your recovery. If you wait longer than two weeks, though, you're procrastinating. Don't allow yourself to ignore this problem, and don't think it will just go away on its own—it won't! Give yourself a good, positive pep talk, then build up your courage and get a trusted adult involved.

Whether you choose to tell your parents first is up to you. You could start with your coach, a school counselor, a teacher, another relative, or by calling a hotline. The important thing is to start somewhere. Below are tips on talking to your parents as well as seeking professional help.

HOW TO TELL YOUR PARENTS

At some point during their teenage years, most people experience tension in their relationship with their parents. This is due in part to the normal letting-go process that accompanies the transition to adulthood. In some ways, teens are self-sufficient and capable of making their own decisions, but in other ways they are still very much in need of their parents' guidance. The difficulty comes in recognizing the difference between a situation you can handle yourself and one with which you need your parents to help you. Dealing with an eating disorder is an example of something you can't do alone, but unfortunately, many parents are ill-equipped to help their children in this area.

I have been bingeing and purging for three years now, and I finally told my parents a couple weeks ago. They seemed to want to help me then, but now whenever I mention it they ignore me or get mad. One time my mother even said I was just doing this to get attention. I'm out of control and I know I need help, but I can't make myself stop on my own. I'm starting to wonder now if they really even care. How can I make them understand?

If you have an eating disorder, you do need the love and support of your family to help you overcome it, but you also must take some responsibility in helping them to help you. Knowing how they might react to your news will help you remain calm when you talk to them.

⊙ Anger. It is common and normal for parents to be angry at the situation, at themselves, and unfortunately even at their child when confronted with the news of an eating disorder. If this happens, remind yourself that they are probably most angry with themselves. They may say things like "Where did we go wrong?" or "Why are you doing this to us?," statements that could easily put you on the defensive, but try your best not to get angry yourself. Since most eating disorders develop at a time of upheaval and change in the life of the sufferer, it is very possible that yours was triggered by a family problem, but now is not the time to place blame. You don't have to give a reason for your problem—just tell them that it exists and you need their help to overcome it. Give them time to cool off, then choose a time when everyone is calm and relaxed to talk to them about how they can help you.

⊙ Sadness. Your parents will probably be very sad for you, for themselves, and for the family in general when you bring them your news. They may cry or apologize for not being better parents. They may even experience a temporary depression and express feelings of hopelessness, saying things like "Your life is ruined" or "How can we ever get through this?" If they do react this way, you will probably feel overwhelming guilt for causing them grief, but do not allow that guilt to stop you from asking for help. It would be natural for you to resolve to take care of your problem on your own in order to spare them the pain of seeing you suffer, but you must resist this impulse. No one's life is perfect, and no child is problem-free. Remember that your parents are there to help you when you need them, no matter how much it may hurt them. Reassure them that you will all get through this and things will be better—your life is not ruined—but for now, you must allow them to share your burden.

⊙ Fear. Another possibility is that your parents will become very frightened. They may even say things like "I can't handle this" or "This is too much for me." Single parents may find helping a child with an eating disorder even more challenging because they have no one to help them work through their own feelings. Consequently, they may turn to their children for the emotional support that a spouse would provide, further burdening the child at an already difficult time. If this is your situation, remember that you are the child, not the parent. You should not have to shoulder the responsibility of "fixing" this yourself. If your parent or parents seem unable to cope with your problem and are depending on you for emotional support, get another adult involved. A person who cares about you but is not as close to you as your parents is less likely to be paralyzed with fear and may be better able to help you.

⊙ Silence. Many people cannot find the words to express their feelings, so they simply say nothing. If your parents react this way, it does not mean that they don't care or that they don't love you. It could be that they just don't know what to say, or perhaps are afraid that they will say the wrong thing and hurt you. After you have found the courage to talk to them about your problem, this reaction will probably be very frustrating for you. If you feel you're not getting through face-to-face, try writing them a letter. This will allow you to clarify your thoughts and to say everything you want to say, and it will allow them time to absorb your words and to choose exactly what they want to say, or write, in response. In your letter, be sure to explain the ways in which your parents can help you, and ask them to give you a response within a certain amount of time (for example, within three days). Tell them that you know this is difficult for them, but it is a serious problem that won't just go away and you are counting on them to help you.

- ⊙ Embarrassment. Some people believe in keeping family members' problems within the family and not "airing their dirty laundry" by telling others. If your parents are this way, they might tell you not to discuss your eating disorder with anyone else. They may imply or even flat-out say that you should be ashamed of it and that if other people find out they will think less of you. This attitude is wrong—keeping problems and feelings to yourself is not healthy and expressing them is nothing to be ashamed of—but if your parents feel this way you will have a hard time convincing them of that. As long as you know that an eating disorder is not shameful, you can cooperate with your parents so they will get you the help you need by not discussing your problem with neighbors, clergy members at your local place of worship, or teachers or other school officials. If your parents' attitude enables you to see the doctors and therapists and other professionals you need to help you begin to recover, you may have to live with it. However, if your parents forbid you to discuss your problem with anyone AND they fail to get help for you, then you will have to go against their wishes and take matters into your own hands. An eating disorder is an extremely serious threat to your health; if your parents refuse to help you, you must find someone else who will, like a teacher, school counselor, coach, or another relative. Keep in mind, however, that this may only be their first reaction; Give them a few days to cool off and approach them again—and you may find that they have changed their minds and want to help you.

⊙ Disbelief. This reaction may be even more likely if you are an athlete. Your parents probably see you as healthy and strong, and may simply refuse to believe that you could have an eating disorder. If this happens, remember that eating disorders are emotional, not physical, problems. Explain to your parents that the physical symptoms of an eating disorder are often harder to see in athletes, but that the problem is there nonetheless and you need their help to overcome it. If their denial is based on assumptions about athletes in general and not a part of one of the reactions discussed here, then showing them this book or having them talk to your doctor or another knowledgeable professional will probably be enough to make them realize the seriousness of the situation.

If days or weeks go by after you've told your parents about your problem and they are still unable to get past their initial reaction, it's time to go to another adult. Telling a trusted guidance counselor, coach, teacher, or doctor would be a good choice, and enlisting the help of another close relative may be an option as well. The important thing is that you find someone to help you. Your wellness is the top priority, and you must do whatever it takes to connect with the people who can help you begin to get better.

HOW TO GET PROFESSIONAL HELP

At various points in your healing process, you may need to enlist the help of a professional with experience in assisting sufferers of eating disorders. Now, you may think that no one can possibly know what this is like for you, and you are right: No one can know exactly what it feels like to be you. But that does not mean that no one can help you. There are many people who want to help people like you, and they have educated themselves in the facts of your illness and have talked to many others in circumstances similar to yours. Although they may not have experienced an eating disorder themselves, they can empathize with you because they have taken the time to learn about the feelings that you're likely to be feeling and the thoughts you're likely to be having. They understand that you are frightened and feel out of control. They see their role in your recovery as that of a guide to needed information and a trusted confidante who will listen without judging and advise without dictating.

There are many different types of professionals who can help you. People who work in the mental health field—psychiatrists, psychologists, counselors, and therapists—are trained to be good listeners. They can help you sort out your feelings and find the underlying cause for your eating disorders. Then you can work together to overcome it, to change it if possible (for example, a negative body image), and to deal with it if you can't change it (for example, your parents' divorce). Medical professionals such as doctors, nutritionists, and dietitians

HOW DO I TELL MY COACH?

The key is to make sure your coach understands how serious your eating disorder is. Now, if your coach has been pushing you to lose weight and train past your body's abilities, it may be impossible to make him or her see the harm that these methods have caused you. It's up to you whether you want to try to educate your coach, but it is crucial to remember that if he or she tries to tell you that you don't really have a problem, that it's not a big deal, or that you're lazy or a quitter, you must get away from that coach's influence immediately! Be sure to tell your parents, counselor, or doctor about the coach's attitude; such pressuring can make it impossible for you to recover.

Luckily, most coaches are not blind to the seriousness of eating disorders, and most do not believe in winning at any cost. Many schools require their physical education instructors to have knowledge of eating disorders, to be able to spot telltale signs, and to discourage unhealthy practices such as rapid weight cutting, overtraining, and radical dieting. People who teach others how to excel in sports are generally interested in the best ways to maintain a healthy body, and they encourage those in their care to push themselves to their limits, but not beyond. So, if your coach is a compassionate person who cares about you, he or she will be concerned for your health and will be willing to help you overcome your eating disorder, even if that means that the team's record may suffer. The coach will also "run interference" for you with your teammates, making sure that you are not ostracized for training or playing less. He or she should be willing to respect your privacy if you prefer not to tell your teammates about your eating disorder, but if you are willing to share, you and your coach together can provide valuable information to the team. You may be able to help others find the courage to seek help for their own disordered eating, and you may help prevent a similar problem in a friend.

can advise you on how to develop healthy eating habits, including choosing the right foods and getting all of your needed nutrients from the foods you eat. People who specialize in fitness, including coaches, trainers, aerobics instructors, and physical therapists, are a good source of information if you want to develop a new exercise program or modify the one you already have. A good fitness expert will emphasize the overall health of your body and will encourage you to set realistic goals in three areas: cardiovascular fitness, strength, and flexibility. He or she will warn you not to push beyond your body's limits and not to use artificial means such as steroids or supplements other than a simple multi-vitamin, and will stress the importance of enjoying physical activity while staying safe and not overdoing it. Taken together, the advice of these very different advisors will provide you with a strong knowledge base upon which to build your strong, healthy body.

Finally, since most eating disorders stem from changes in the life of the victim, family counseling is often very helpful in stabilizing the sufferer's environment and educating parents and siblings in what the eating disorder is, why it developed, and how to help the sufferer overcome it.

If you are unsure of where to begin looking for help, a good first step is to call a hotline or visit a Web site that offers

If you are unsure of where to begin looking for help, a good first step is to call a hotline or visit a Web site that offers referrals in your area.

referrals in your area. There are many hotline numbers, Web sites, and other service organizations
listed in the Where to Go for Help section of this
book. The people who answer hotlines are trained
to listen to your problems without even knowing
who you are and to give you referrals to professionals in your area who can offer long-term, personal-
ized help. Hotline workers are often
volunteers—they do this work because they want to
help people, not just to make money. They are
interested in giving you the support and information
you need to begin your recovery.

WHAT WILL TREATMENT BE LIKE?

There are a number of different approaches to treating eating disorders. The best one for you should be
based on the severity of your condition as well as
your individual personality and the circumstances
that brought about the problem in the first place.
Since anorexia, bulimia, BED, and compulsive
exercise are psychological illnesses but cause
physical problems, you will most likely want to
involve professionals from both the medical and
mental health fields in your care.

If you are extremely ill, the first step might be
spending some time in a hospital to stabilize your
physical condition. If so, you can work out a step-
by-step plan for your recovery while you're there,
and you will probably meet many different people
who can help you both in planning what to do and
in carrying it out. Steps in your physical recovery
may include visiting your primary care physician
or family doctor to assess the damage to your

DRUGS AND EATING DISORDER TREATMENT

Some mental health professionals use antidepressants as a tool in treating an eating disorder. Since a person suffering from an eating disorder also often shows signs of depression, it is theorized that treating the depression with drugs such as Prozac, Zoloft, Paxil, or Elavil may also help alleviate the eating disorder. The drug alone will not bring about a cure, however; therapy is still needed to work through the emotional problems that led to the eating disorder, but the drug may allow the patient to get more out of the therapy process. Not all therapists can prescribe medication: psychiatrists can, but psychologists cannot. When seeking treatment, be prepared to decide whether you would be comfortable including the use of an antidepressant in your recovery. If you decide to try it, ask questions about its possible side effects and learn as much as you can about what the drug is expected to do for you.

body and decide how to repair it. If you are bulimic, a trip to the dentist is a good idea to. Your dentist can give you a thorough exam and reverse any decay that may have begun as a result of purging. Another element in your physical healing is educating yourself in healthy eating habits. You may be referred to a dietitian or nutritionist for help in learning how to eat well and exercise in moderation to maintain a healthy body.

Your most difficult task will probably be your mental and emotional healing. This side of your recovery will most likely involve some sort of therapy, which may be one-on-one or together with your family members or others recovering from eating disorders. You may find that a combined approach—some individual sessions with a psychiatrist or psychologist combined with some family counseling and perhaps some group therapy or participation in a self-help group—will give you a good variety of useful insight. Whichever approach will be the most comfortable and effective for you is the best one to use.

There is no predictable time frame for recovery from disordered eating. If you are in the beginning stages, you may be able to turn it around in a matter of weeks, but don't be discouraged if you find that your course of treatment is expected to take many months. Eating disorders do not appear overnight; they grow slowly over time, and when you do finally realize that you have a problem, many facets of your life have already been changed and influenced by it. Therefore, an eating disorder cannot be cured overnight; it will take time for you to break old habits and train yourself to think and act in new, self-affirming ways.

WHAT IF I'M NOT RICH?

It is true that professional help can be expensive. If you have no insurance, or if your insurance won't cover it and paying for such services is a problem for your family, there are low-cost and free programs to help you; they may be harder to find or may take longer to get into, but don't give up. Remember that overcoming your eating disorder is crucial to your health, so keep trying until you get help.

REMEMBER, THEY'RE HUMAN TOO

When you seek the services of a professional, whether it's a doctor, therapist, nutrition counselor, or trainer, remember that that person is a fallible human being just like yourself. Experts can make mistakes, and they can exercise poor judgment. It's okay for you to disagree with them or to question their reasons or sources of information. It is important for you to take an active role in healing yourself, and if someone advises you to do something that you think is wrong or that makes you uncomfortable, speak up. Discuss your discomfort. If the advisor becomes defensive and demands that you follow his or her orders, consider finding someone else to help you.

(It may help to discuss the situation with your parents.) There are extreme cases where people must be hospitalized and treated against their will in order to keep them alive, but such situations are rare. In most cases, you will be allowed to have a voice in choosing the course of your treatment, and if you are truly committed to healing, the adults who are helping you should allow you to direct your recovery. If you feel that you are not being heard, speak up, and if you still aren't taken seriously, find someone else to help you.

A FRIEND IN NEED:
HELPING OTHERS PREVENT OR
DEAL WITH AN EATING DISORDER

I have never forgotten the time in elementary school when a classmate of mine told our group of girls what her mother had said to her at dinner the night before. I forget how the subject came up, but I remember that she seemed stunned and very sad as she told us about it. It seems that her mother had made chicken and dumplings for dinner, and our friend asked for more. Her mother told her harshly that she was already too fat and didn't need another dumpling. I remember looking at her and thinking, My God, if she is fat, what am I? It has been over twenty years since this happened, but I have always wished that I had known what to say to that girl, and I have always wondered what became of her.

Often it is hard to know what to say when something like the above scenario happens. Many people

SOME QUESTIONS TO ASK WHEN CHOOSING A THERAPIST

The American Anorexia/Bulimia Association suggests asking the following questions when choosing a therapist to help you toward recovery from an eating disorder:

About the Therapist:

- ⊙ How did you get involved in treating eating disorders?

- ⊙ What percentage of your clients have eating disorders?

- ⊙ How much time will we spend focusing on food, weight, and diet issues?

- ⊙ Will you allow me to come to an appointment even if I have a relapse (binge/purge, overexercise, and so on)?

- ⊙ Do you believe that people with eating disorders can be cured, or will I always have this disease?

- ⊙ What things should I know about you? Why should I see you?

About the Therapy Process:

⊙ How would you describe your approach to therapy?

⊙ What goals will we set?

⊙ Will you involve my family in my recovery?

⊙ Will you monitor my weight and what I eat?

⊙ What can I expect during a session? How long will each session be, and how often will we meet?

⊙ What do I have to accomplish for you to consider me recovered?

⊙ Do you accept my insurance? Do you charge for cancellations?

⊙ What days and hours are you available for appointments? Can I call you between appointments, and if so is there a charge for that?

are afraid of saying the wrong thing, but they can't imagine what the right thing to say would be, so they simply say nothing. Think back to a time when you told someone about something hurtful that happened to you and the other person didn't say anything. Did you feel heard? Did you feel that the other person cared about you? Most likely you felt ignored or rejected. The other person may have felt terrible for you, but that sympathy didn't do you any good because he or she couldn't express it. If you suspect a friend or family member is suffering from an eating disorder, find the courage to talk to him or her about it. It is better to say something in a clumsy way than to remain silent, waiting for the perfect words to come into your head. Similarly, it is better to bring up the subject yourself rather than waiting for him or her to mention it or for the best possible moment, although you should try to do it at a time when your friend is calm and not in a hurry to be somewhere or to finish something. Some other tips for getting a friend to talk about an eating disorder include:

- ⊙ Be ready to give your friend factual information about eating disorders and/or compulsive exercise. It may help to have this book with you; offer to lend it to him or her.

- ⊙ Avoid attacking or accusing. Use "I" statements instead of "you" statements; for example, "I've noticed that you seem to throw up a lot. Is there something wrong?" instead of "You throw up all the time, so obviously you are bulimic."

⊙ Practice "empathic listening." This means listening with just one intention: to understand what your friend is telling you and how he or she feels about it. Many people make the mistake of using the time during which the other person is talking to think about what they want to say next. But when you're thinking your own thoughts, you can't really pay attention to what your friend is saying! Another element of empathic listening is validating your friend's words and feelings. You can do this by making eye contact, using your body language to show that you are paying attention, responding with small, encouraging words such as "uh huh" or "I see" or "tell me more," and by resisting the urge to compare yourself to your friend or to talk about similar problems of your own.

⊙ Be ready for rejection. Your friend may not be ready to accept help or to face the reality of his or her problem. He or she may even react with denial or anger. Try not to take these reactions personally; remember that your friend is suffering a great deal of emotional pain and may lash out at you for raising the subject, but isn't really angry with you. Give it some time and eventually your friend may be able to talk to you about it.

HOW CAN I TELL IF MY FRIEND HAS AN EATING DISORDER?

Sometimes eating disorders can be very difficult to detect in others. The victim may feel ashamed of his or her problem and may go to great lengths to hide it from others. However, there are some signs that you may be able to pick up on if you pay close attention. First, review the questions in the box entitled *How Can I Tell If I Have an Eating Disorder or Exercise Compulsion?* in chapter four and apply them to your friend. Then ask yourself:

- Does she seem to be spending more time alone lately?

- Does he always seem to be working out?

- Does she frequently go to the bathroom after a meal?

- Does he have extreme mood swings?

- Have I ever heard her throwing up?

- Does he join in "eating contests" to see which guy can pack in the most food at one time?

- Have I ever noticed pills in her purse or bedroom?

⊙ Has he ever used dangerous weight-cutting methods such as exercising in a sauna or taking water pills?

⊙ Does she have any physical signs such as cuts on her hands or "chipmunk cheeks"?

⊙ Is he obsessed with having huge muscles and a washboard stomach?

⊙ How often do I see her eat? Does she finish her meals?

⊙ Does he use supplements purported to help burn fat, build muscle, or increase energy?

⊙ Does she talk about her body in a negative way, or compare herself unfavorably to me, other friends, or pictures in magazines?

⊙ Is there something happening in his life that could be causing emotional pain?

If any of these questions have you worried for your friend's well-being, find a gentle, caring way to tell him or her about your concerns and offer help.

⊙ Finally, offer to help in any way you can, but don't promise to keep it a secret if your friend refuses to tell a trusted adult. Explain how dangerous an eating disorder is to a person's health, and tell your friend that you care and want to help. Tell him or her that you are always willing to listen and to feel free to talk to you any time about the eating disorder or any other problem. Your friend should feel reassured that you will still be there regardless of what he or she does about the problem.

SOME FINAL THOUGHTS

Now that you've read this book, you have a strong foundation for building healthy attitudes toward sports and their relationship with eating, body image, and self-esteem. Please share what you've learned with friends, family members, teammates, coaches, and classmates, and remember to hold your ground against unrealistic societal and media pressure and people who still have uninformed opinions about eating disorders.

If you have lost someone to an eating disorder, visit the Something Fishy Web site on eating disorders at *http://www.something-fishy.org* and post a tribute to your loved one in the "In Loving Memory" section. Dozens of personal stories appear there, contributed by broken-hearted friends and relatives of eating-disorder victims whose bodies could not withstand the effects of their disease.

Glossary

anorexia nervosa An eating disorder in which one intentionally starves oneself.

binge To consume large amounts of food, often in secret and usually without control.

bulimia nervosa An eating disorder in which one eats normal or large amounts of food and then rids the body of the food by either forcing oneself to vomit, abusing laxatives or diuretics, taking enemas, or exercising obsessively.

calorie A unit to measure the energy-producing value of food.

compulsive eating An eating disorder marked by uncontrollable eating of large amounts of food.

demoralize To bring down someone's morale or self-esteem.

denial Refusal to admit or face the truth or reality of a situation.

depression A state of extreme and prolonged sadness.

deprive To withhold something from or take something away.

indulgent Giving in easily to wants and desires.

inpatient A patient who is treated and remains in a hospital or a clinic for treatment.

internalize To bottle up problems or emotions.

obsessive Excessive to the point of being unreasonable.

outpatient A patient in a clinic or hospital who does not live in the hospital but who visits on a regular basis for treatment.

overachiever A person who strives for success beyond what is expected.

psychiatrist A doctor who is trained to treat people with mental, emotional, or behavioral disorders.

ravenous A state of extreme hunger.

self-esteem Confidence or satisfaction in oneself; self-respect.

Where to Go for Help

In the United States

American Anorexia/Bulimia Association, Inc.
   (AABA)
165 West 46th St., Suite 1108
New York, NY 10036
(212) 575-6200
Web site: http://members.aol.com/amanbu
Committed to increasing public awareness of eating
disorders and providing treatment information and
referrals to sufferers and their families and friends.

Anorexia Nervosa and Related Eating Disorders,
   Inc. (ANRED)
P.O. Box 5102
Eugene, OR 97405
(541) 344-1144

Center for the Study of Anorexia and Bulimia
1 West 91st Street
New York, NY 10024
(212) 595-3449

Eating Disorders Awareness and Prevention
    (EDAP)
603 Stewart Street, Suite 803
Seattle, WA 98101
(206) 382-3587
Web site: http://members.aol.com/edapinc
Dedicated to increasing the awareness and prevention of eating disorders. Sponsor of National
Eating Disorders Awareness Week every February;
provides assistance in organizing local events and
educational programs.

National Association of Anorexia Nervosa and
    Associated Disorders (ANAD)
P.O. Box 7
Highland Park, IL 60035
(847) 831-3438

National Eating Disorders Organization (NEDO)
445 East Grandille Road
Worthington, OH 43085
(918) 481-4044
Web site:http://www.laureate.com/nedointro.html
Provides information on anorexia, bulimia, and binge
eating disorder and on recovery and treatment.

National Institute of Mental Health Eating
    Disorders Program
Building 10, Room 35231
Bethesda, MD 20892
(101) 496-1891

Overeaters Anonymous
(505) 891-2664
Web site: http://www.overeaters.org
Provides information and referrals to local chapters.

Rader Programs
(800) 841-1515
Web site: http://www.raderpro.com/
Offers treatment programs in California, Illinois, and Oklahoma.

The Renfrew Center
(800) RENFREW (800 736-3739)
Web site: http://www.renfrew.org
Provides information on its treatment centers in the United States as well as general information and referrals.

In Canada

Anorexia Nervosa and Bulimia Association
    (ANAB)
(613) 547-3584
Web site: http://www.ams.queensu.ca/anab/
Twenty-four hour crisis and information hotline.

S.A.F.E. (Self-Abuse Finally Ends)
(800) DON'T-CUT (800 366-8288)
http://www.wwdc.com/safe/
Dedicated to reducing the burden of suffering caused by self-abuse. Provides information, support, and treatment programs for victims.

HOTLINES

1-800-THERAPIST Network
(800) 843-7274
Web site: http://www.1-800-therapist.com/
Provides referrals to local therapists for any condition.

Boys Town USA
(800) 448-3000
Hearing Impaired: (800)448-1833
Web site: http://www.ffbh.boystown.org/
Twenty-four hour crisis line for all children—girls
and boys—who need help with any problem.
Parents are also welcome to call. Spanish-speak-
ing counselors and translation service for many
other languages available.

Bulimia and Self-Help Hotline
(314) 588-1683
Twenty-four hour crisis line.

National Mental Health Association Information Center
(800) 969-NMHA (800 969-6642)
Provides referrals to local Mental Health Association
offices, which can refer you to local programs.

WEB SITES

American Anorexia/Bulimia Association, Inc.
    (AABA) homepage.
Web site: http://members.aol.com/amanbu
Contains extensive information on the path to
recovery from anorexia, bulimia, and binge eating
disorder.

American Psychiatric Association Online.
Web site: http://www.psych.org/public_info/
    eating.html
Provides information on anorexia and bulimia,
including an extensive section on their possible
causes.

Anorexia Nervosa and Related Eating Disorders, Inc.
Web site: http://www.anred.com
A nonprofit organization that provides information about anorexia nervosa, bulimia nervosa,
binge eating disorder, compulsive exercising,
and other less well-known food and weight disorders. Includes a section on eating disorders in
males.

Canadian Paediatric Society Adolescent Medicine
    Committee.
Web site: http://www.cps.ca/english/statements/
    AM/am96-04.htm
"Eating Disorders in Adolescents: Principles of
Diagnosis and Treatment." Journal article dis-
cussing the physical and mental effects of eating
disorders and possible barriers to recovery.

Eating Disorders Online
Web site: http://kathy.addr.com
Contains hundreds of links to related sites.

Elliott, K. D.
Web site: http://bewell.com/healthy/man/
    1998/bed/
"BED Confessions." Contains information on binge
eating disorder.

Knowlton, Leslie.
Web site: http://www.mhsource.com/edu/
    psytimes/p950942.html
"Eating Disorders in Males." Discussion of the
impact of anorexia and bulimia on male sufferers.

Larsen, Joanne. "Ask the Dietitian."
http://www.dietitian.com/anorexia.html
Contains questions about anorexia and answers
from the doctor.

Males and Eating Disorders.
Web site: http://www.primenet.com/~danslos/
    males/males.html
Contains personal stories, information, and links to
other useful sites.

Mudgett, Heather.
Web site: http://www.suite101.com/article.cfm/
    eating_disorders/9979
Contains information and links on famous eating-
    disorder victims.

National Institute of Mental Health.
    Web site: http://www.nimh.nih.gov/publicat/
    eatdis.htm
Contains information on anorexia, bulimia, and
binge eating disorder, and includes discussion of
the theorized link between depression and eating
disorders.

The Something Fishy Web Site on Eating
    Disorders.
Web site: http://www.something-fishy.org
Huge collection of information, true stories, help
sources, music, remembrances of deceased sufferers, links, and empowering support. Sponsors live
chat events with guests whose lives have been
impacted by eating disorders.

University of Florida Counseling Center.
Web site: http://www.ufsa.ufl.edu/Counsel/
    text.html
"Body Acceptance and Eating Disorders." Contains several scored quizzes as well and information and self-help suggestions.

University of Minnesota Duluth Counseling Services.
Web site: http://www.d.umn.edu/hlthserv/
    counseling/eating_disorder.html
A scored checklist to evaluate yourself for an eating disorder.

For Further Reading

Andersen, Arnold E. *Males with Eating Disorders.* New York: Brunner/Mazel, 1990.

Apostolides, Marianne. *Inner Hunger: A Young Woman's Struggle through Anorexia and Bulimia.* New York: W. W. Norton & Co., 1998.

Barr, Linda. *Emily's Secret: No One Can Find Out* (fiction). St. Petersburg, FL: Willowisp Press/Pages Press, 1997.

Bode, Janet. *Food Fight: A Guide to Eating Disorders for Preteens and Their Parents.* New York: Simon & Schuster, 1997.

Cooper, Peter J. *Bulimia Nervosa & Binge-Eating: A Guide to Recovery.* New York: New York University Press, 1995.

Davis, Brangien. *What's Real, What's Ideal: Overcoming a Negative Body Image.* New York: The Rosen Publishing Group, 1999.

Hall, Liza F. *Perk! The Story of a Teenager with Bulimia.* Carlsbad, CA: Gurze Designs&Books, 1997.

Harmon, Dan, and Carol C Nadelson. *Anorexia Nervosa: Starving for Attention.* Broomall, PA: Chelsea House, 1998.

111

Hollis, Judi. *Fat Is a Family Affair: A Guide for People with Eating Disorders and Those Who Love Them.* Center City, MN: Hazelden, 1996.

Katherine, Anne. *Anatomy of a Food Addiction: The Brain Chemistry of Overeating.* Carlsbad, CA: Gurze Designs&Books, 1997.

Kolodny, Nancy J. *When Food's a Foe: How You Can Confront and Conquer Your Eating Disorder.* Boston, MA: Little, Brown & Co., 1998.

Krasnow, Michael. *My Life as a Male Anorexic.* Binghamton, NY: Haworth Press, 1996.

Levenkron, Steven. *Treating and Overcoming Anorexia Nervosa.* New York: Warner Books, 1997.

Pipher, Mary. *Reviving Ophelia: Saving the Selves of Adolescent Girls.* New York: Ballantine Books, 1995.

Poulton, Terry. *No Fat Chicks: How Big Business Profits by Making Women Hate Their Bodies—And How to Fight Back.* New York: Birch Lane Press, 1997.

Prussin, Rebecca; Philip Harvey, and Theresa Foy Digeronimo. *Hooked on Exercise: How to Understand and Manage Exercise Addiction.* New York: Fireside, 1992.

Sacker, Ira M., Ara M. Sacker, and Marc A. Zimmer, *Dying to Be Thin: Understanding & Defeating Anorexia & Bulimia.* New York: Warner Books, 1995.

Sandbeck, Terence J. *The Deadly Diet: Recovering from Anorexia and Bulimia.* Oakland, CA: New Harbinger Publications, 1993.

Sheppard, Kay. *Food Addiction: The Body Knows.* Deerfield Beach, FL: Health Communications, 1993.

Thompson, Ron A., and Roberta Trattner Sherman, *Helping Athletes with Eating Disorders.* Champaign, IL: Human Kinetics Publications, 1992.

Wolf, Naomi. *The Beauty Myth: How Images of Beauty Are Used against Women.* New York: Anchor, 1992.

Yates, Alayne. *Compulsive Exercise and the Eating Disorders: Toward an Integrated Theory of Activity.* New York: Brunner/Mazel, 1991.

Index